THE ANCIENT WORLD

IDEAS IN PROFILE
SMALL INTRODUCTIONS TO BIG TOPICS

THE
ANCIENT
WORLD

JERRY TONER

P

PROFILE BOOKS

First published in Great Britain in 2015 by
PROFILE BOOKS LTD
3 Holford Yard
Bevin Way
London WC1X 9HD
www.profilebooks.com

Copyright © Jerry Toner 2015

10 9 8 7 6 5 4 3 2 1

Designed by Jade Design *www.jadedesign.co.uk*

Maps by Martin Lubikowski, ML Design
www.facebook.com/makingmapswork

Printed and bound in Italy by L.E.G.O. S.p.A.

A CIP catalogue record for this book is available from the British Library.

ISBN 978 1 78125 420 2
eISBN 978 1 78283 141 9

CONTENTS

1

ANOTHER ANCIENT WORLD

What was it like to walk through Rome? Rome: the imperial city of a million people, bigger than any western city until the industrial revolution. What would we have seen? Gleaming white classical temples and toga-clad Romans? Cicero delivering his speeches in the forum? Or if we strolled through Athens would we have found Socrates goading the other Athenians by pointing out the errors in their logic? Would we have been able to take our eyes off the glory of the Parthenon? This book has no intention of introducing you to these hackneyed images of the ancient past.

Imagine an alternative ancient world. What do we encounter as we stroll through an ancient city? For a start, our senses get a totally different experience. The stench from garbage and human excrement hits us hard. For all the Romans' impressive developments in sewers, these are confined to the main public areas in the city. Away from them, people dump wherever they can. The city's slaves and manual labourers clear away some of this waste and take it to pits outside the city walls. But the smell still permeates the air.

Death fills the air too. Many of the homeless die in the street. Even emperors can be affected by this. Vespasian was once having his dinner when a dog ran in from the street and dropped a human hand under the table. This is a pre-industrial world where attitudes to waste and physical remains are different to ours. That does not mean that the ancients take no care with dead bodies. Far from it. Like the heroes of the *Iliad*, they are desperate to have a proper burial, even if this means simply a handful of dust thrown over their corpse. In Rome, where cremation is the more usual form of disposal, bodies are taken outside the city limits and burnt on simple pyres. A city of Rome's size produces a steady supply of the dead. Perhaps a hundred per day were incinerated along the roads that led into the city. The smell of burning flesh welcomes the traveller to the grim realities of life in an ancient town.

Tourists visiting the sights of the ancient world today generally adopt the reverent hushed tones reserved for places of worship. In the Colosseum, visitors stand quietly out of respect for the many thousands who perished there. There's nothing wrong with this. It makes us think about how different the past was. It shows that it matters to us not to disrespect these long-dead people. But it gives us a very false sense of what it was like to live in these places. The noise could be deafening. The cheers of the crowd in the amphitheatre and the Circus Maximus, where about a quarter of a million spectators could squeeze in, rang out over the city. Wooden carts clattered over the stone streets, hawkers shouted out to advertise their wares using distinct types of cry depending on what they were selling, and drovers herded the thousands of animals needed to help feed the city to the butchers who slaughtered them.

Many things were not as they now seem. We gaze at the cool, white marble of the ancient statues of the Parthenon and its simplicity symbolises the purity of the ancient world. The Greeks were the people who invented reason and science, who were able to look beneath the surface appearance of things and understand them for what they were. In fact, most if not all ancient statues were painted. Or they were gilded or glazed or varnished. The main features of the face were highlighted to make them stand out for the viewer. Eyes were painted white or inset with coloured glass to make them as lifelike as possible. Lips were exaggerated with dramatic reds like some ancient form of collagen implanting. And the more important the statue, the bolder and more expensive the colouring. Red cinnabars and Egyptian blues, for example, were used to give a sense of the divine power of a godlike emperor. If you see a mock-up of how an ancient statue actually looked, it's hard today not to regard it as garish. Contemporaries would have seen it as close to divine reality. This just shows how difficult it is to view the ancient world as they did. We have become so accustomed to this world through films, paintings or neoclassical architecture that we

A painted reconstruction of a statue from the Temple of Aphaea on Aegina

may be tempted to believe that if we went there in a time machine we'd feel pretty much at home. If I'm going to do one thing in this short book, it will be to challenge this sense of familiarity.

As the multicoloured statue makes clear, if we went back to the ancient world we wouldn't even be able to trust our senses. We have learnt to see things in certain ways. We might hear the same noises as the ancient locals but we would understand them differently. Smells that would disgust us were quite normal in the ancient world – we would have to completely retrain our senses before we could even begin to experience it in the same way as its inhabitants.

We imagine that we experience the senses as five separate phenomena, each with its own particular characteristics. But the ancients mixed up the senses to create a complex and overlapping descriptive palette. Homer's famous image of the 'wine-dark sea' related not just to its colour but also to its sharp, pungent taste and smell. Perhaps it hinted at what being at sea felt like – the woozy feeling of having drunk too much. The idea of tasting, smelling and feeling colours is not something we easily understand. Even reading was a varied sensory activity. Texts were designed not just to be read but also to be heard, partly because literacy levels were low. It seemed natural to taste, hear and smell what to us might appear as purely visual descriptions. Good writing allowed the audience to experience by means of words.

Just how low literacy levels were is unclear. Perhaps as few as five per cent of the population were functionally literate, meaning they knew enough words to be able to communicate in a simple written form or read basic texts. The numbers who could read the literature of high culture were even smaller: a couple of per cent at most. Education was expensive and most people needed to get their children working at a young age. A lot of what we regard as classical culture is the high culture of this small group of the rich. Only the wealthy could afford to idle their time away in reading poetry or learning the finer points of prose composition. In fact, it was the very uselessness of such activities that made them attractive to the upper classes in society, in the same way that learning Latin often does today. This doesn't mean that no one else in society could enjoy good poetry. Both Homer and Virgil could be widely appreciated precisely because they were designed to be read out loud. Public performances, whether in the formal environment of the stage or more informal recitations in the forum, were popular. Nor does it mean that the classics of literature, which form the core of a traditional Classics course, are any less valuable or worth studying. But it does mean that if we want to get a clearer picture of the ancient world as a whole we need to expand our horizons significantly away from this highly literate group.

The wealth gap in the ancient world was massive. The minimum property qualification for a Roman senator was one million sesterces, which could have fed about two thousand families for a year. The super-rich had colossal fortunes. Crassus, the man who bankrolled Julius Caesar's rise to power, was estimated to be worth close to 200 million. After he died invading Persia in an attempt to emulate Caesar's military achievements, the Persians poured molten gold down his corpse's throat as a symbol of his great thirst for money. Comparing wealth across the ages is an impossible task. What made the ancient rich seem particularly distant from the ordinary folk was the absence of any middle class, in the modern sense of an economically powerful group with their own distinctive culture and values. Theirs was not a capitalist system, nor did a system of fractional banking exist to facilitate credit creation. Wealth meant land and property and it was far more difficult for people to acquire the capital needed to buy them. A few lucky ones made enough money to rival the top echelons of society. Most people, though, lived in a world where acquiring a trade or a skill, such as barbering or butchery, represented the best way to improve their quality of life.

What helped bridge this huge wealth gap was a social expectation that the rich and powerful would share some of their good fortune with ordinary citizens. Whether it was providing subsidised bread, paying for shows in the theatres, putting on animal hunts and gladiatorial combats in the arenas, hosting public banquets or building grand bath houses, the ancient political elites gave many ordinary citizens, especially in the city of Rome during the empire, the means to enjoy regular tastes of the good life. 'Bread and circuses' came to sit at the heart of the mutually beneficial arrangement whereby emperors rewarded the Roman people for their continued support. It shows just how much importance ordinary people placed on the ability to have some fun as well as on having enough to eat. No doubt the harshness of everyday life made the entertainments feel all the more gratifying and enjoyable.

The ancient world was male-dominated. Only men could vote or hold political office. Women were expected to be subservient to their husbands, daughters obedient to their fathers. When women like Agrippina did wield behind-the-scenes power in the imperial palace it only served to show how inappropriate it was for a woman to do so. Her ruthless pursuit of power for her son Nero – she is even alleged to have murdered her husband, the emperor Claudius, with a dish of deadly mushrooms – served to emphasise that she possessed the very opposite qualities to those considered desirable in a Roman woman. One tombstone records a husband's praise for his dead wife: 'pure, loyal, loving, dutiful, she did what she was told'. It was everything a man looked for in a wife. Almost all of the surviving texts were written by men for men. How do we give voice to the fifty per cent of ancients who were women?

The ancient population was also young. But young did not necessarily mean healthy. An ancient had a life expectancy at birth of not much more than twenty-five years. It's about three times as high in the western world today. Poor sanitation, lack of basic hygiene and limited medical knowledge all combined to make death a regular caller in the average household. 'At birth' is the key phrase here. Infants bore the brunt of this onslaught. About a third of all babies died in their first year of life. About half of all children were dead before their fifth birthday. If you made it past these vulnerable first few years then the outlook improved significantly. Make it to ten and you could reasonably expect to live into your fifties. Not many made it to what we would think of as retirement age. Grandparents were a rarity, absent parents and orphans commonplace. The old image of the ancient household with the all-powerful father at its head should be revised, given the harsh reality that many fathers would have died young through illness, disease or warfare. High infant mortality placed a huge burden on women to have children. The average woman needed to have five or six live births just to keep the population stable. Society made sure that its womenfolk had babies young. One tombstone refers to a woman named Veturia who died after sixteen years of marriage at the ripe old age of twenty-seven. Five of her six children had died before her. Eleven was a young age at which to get married, even by ancient standards. But by their mid- to late teens, most girls had been married off to a significantly older man in what amounted to a marriage arranged by their fathers or, if the father was dead, by uncles or brothers.

Ancient society was dominated by men but its population consisted mostly of outsiders and other marginal people. Even among the men, only a minority had any rights. We think of Athens as the birthplace of democracy. Yet of a total population in Athens and its surrounding territory of about two hundred and fifty thousand, only about thirty thousand were citizens. The figure had been closer to sixty thousand but the great statesman Pericles had made the qualifications even more difficult to meet. This left only about 10 to 15 per cent of the population of Athens entitled to vote. To be sure, the degree of democracy that operated among this small group was radical and direct: each individual citizen could propose and vote on legislation – there was none of this 'representation' nonsense; people were expected to make up their own mind. Elections were distrusted because they always ended up with the rich and powerful buying the electorate's votes – random selection was thought to be the truly democratic process (as juries are still chosen today). But the enfranchised section of society was tiny by our standards and governed by blind prejudices based on gender, ethnicity and birth.

Slaves made up a large part of the population. How many slaves there were in the ancient world is actually very hard to assess. The evidence we have is thin. In any case, the numbers will have varied dramatically from place to place and period to period. Athens and Roman Italy were two of the great slave-owning societies in world history. They sucked in slaves from their empires who were then used to work the land and the mines and serve at table. Slaves made up something like 20 per cent of the population of Italy. In Rome, the slaves were everywhere – about a third of the population.

What is amazing is that the locals hardly noticed them. We have no equivalent of *Twelve Years a Slave* or other first-hand accounts of what it was like to be a slave in the ancient world. Slavery was absolutely normal. It was a basic institution that everybody took for granted. There was no abolition movement and no one ever talked about such a possibility. Owning a slave was as normal as owning a fridge is today. If we went to an ancient city, I think the presence of slaves would stand out strongly for us. Whether scurrying along to the market to buy food or carrying their master to the forum, slaves were the workhorses of antiquity. Their widespread use takes us to the heart of the difference between our world and that of the ancients.

The casual brutality shown towards slaves could be shocking. The emperor Hadrian, generally thought of as a good emperor, was once disturbed by a slave while writing a letter. In an imperial hissy fit he poked one of the slave's eyes out with his pen. Now, being a 'good' emperor, Hadrian actually apologised to the slave and asked what he could do to make it up to him. The slave simply replied that no gift could ever make up for the loss of an eye. The emperor was left upset, not because he had blinded a man, but because he had let his temper get the better of him. OK, this is a high-profile story that probably doesn't bear much relationship to the daily reality of slave life. But other evidence shows that the violence was almost more disturbing because of its very routineness. One inscription lists the prices charged by a kind of municipal punishment service. Want your slave flogged, tortured or crucified but don't want to get your own hands dirty? Then call in the experts. For the price of a few pounds of bread, someone would come to your house and do the dirty deed. They were even thoughtful enough to bring their own gibbets for flogging and nails for crucifixion. Hot pitch could be supplied if required for the purposes of torture.

Some punishment could be almost comically cruel. A rich Roman called Vedius Pollio once invited his friend, the emperor Augustus, around for dinner. The entertainment was briefly interrupted when one of the host's young slaves broke a valuable crystal cup. Trying to impress the emperor with his toughness, Vedius ordered the slave boy to be taken and thrown to the large eels (some say they were lampreys) that he kept in his fish pond. But Augustus was

The punishment of a slave

not impressed. In fact, he was outraged at this novel form of cruelty. He ordered Vedius to free the slave and he told the other slaves to bring all the crystal cups they could find and smash them in their master's presence. He then told Vedius to fill in the fish pond and get rid of the eels.

But what this remarkable story really shows us is that we would be wrong to think the ancients always treated their slaves with such exquisite brutality. Most people, like Augustus, thought such bizarre cruelty was shocking. When it came to getting the best from them, owners understood that their slaves could not simply be terrified into working hard. Instead, a variety of techniques were used, from bonuses to the hope of future freedom, to incentivise slaves to work productively and willingly. Slaves were also an investment. They cost a lot of money – probably enough to feed a family of four for two years – and treating them badly simply damaged the value of your assets and reduced the return they could be expected to produce.

Unlike the Greeks, the Romans had an inclusive attitude to outsiders. Good slaves, particularly domestic slaves who had direct contact with their master, were rewarded with their freedom and could become citizens. Similarly, when the Romans conquered they would, over time, assimilate some of their subjects and their practices. This had the great advantage of making the Roman citizenry, and hence the army, expand in line with its conquests. There was no natural limit to how far it could conquer because it Romanised those it brought into its empire. But we would be wrong to think of the Roman empire as a uniform society. Yes, there were amphitheatres in many provinces (although they were primarily in the west, where 252 of the 272 known examples have been found). And yes, Roman villas dotted the countryside (but these were built by the local aristocracies). The reality on the ground was that the Roman empire encompassed many different forms of culture, ranging from the ordinary people of England (the nasty little Brits, as one Roman calls them) to groups like the Jews and Syrians who refused to be fully Romanised. This wasn't simply an act of resistance. The Roman empire was a multicultural entity where people adopted different identities depending on the situation they found themselves in. When dealing with the government they might emphasise their Roman citizenship or their loyalty to the cult of the emperor. When involved in local politics, though, they would speak the local language and highlight their network of small-town contacts. When the local rulers met with each other, they often used a shared education in the classics of Greek and Latin literature in order to establish common ground. Any account of the ancient world is going to have to include a look at this mosaic of cultural identities.

Religion was everywhere. But religion meant much more than the traditional pantheon of gods sitting atop Mount Olympus. The state-sponsored cults of both Greece and Rome did focus on these mainstream deities but they represented only a part of the picture. The ancient world provided a religious supermarket for the worshipper to choose from according to his or her purposes. They might want to have their horoscopes read and so visit an astrologer. Or they might want to consult the gods about the kinds of daily problems they faced and therefore call on a diviner. One set of questions, known as the Oracles of Astrampsychus, lists ninety-two of these everyday dilemmas. 'Will I be set free?' asks a worried slave; 'Will I see a death?' asks someone else, perhaps the spouse of a sick person. 'Will I inherit?' asks another, fearing, perhaps, that their assiduous attempts to ingratiate themselves with an elderly relative will not yield the desired rewrite of the will. Perhaps the worshipper has had a worrying dream and wants to consult a dream-interpreter to see what the gods are trying to tell him in his sleep. Another might be terrified that her baby is being cursed by a hostile neighbour and will thus pay a magician to cast a spell in order to counteract its effect. To colour this variety, the many forms of local, provincial gods need to be added to the mix.

A walk down the average ancient street would have bombarded us with all kinds of religious imagery:

household gods painted on the doors; wind chimes in the form of deformed dwarfs to keep evil spirits at bay; derogatory drawings of a donkey-headed Jesus being crucified. Religion was not neatly encapsulated by the church at the end of the road, a place to enter once a week at most – or, more likely, for the occasional big event – and nor was it cut off from secular society. Religion pervaded everything in the ancient world, from Greek theatre to taverns to public sacrifices to religious processions before the games: nothing could take place without the approval of the gods. It was a world where atheism was almost unimaginable.

Some of the acts of piety would really disturb us. To worship the Great Mother, the priest stood in a hole covered by a grate. Dressed in a silk cloak and wearing a gold crown, he waited while a bull, itself beautified with decorations of flowers and gold ornaments, was slaughtered above him. The bull's blood poured through the grate onto the priest below who welcomed it onto his face, even allowing it to fill his open mouth. Blood-soaked, he then came up out of the trench and stood before his flock of fellow worshippers, pure and reborn. He had been baptised in a blood bath. The similarities with Christian baptism are as obvious as the differences. The aim was a symbolic rebirth, the means using a more literal life force than the symbolic washing of water. It's no surprise that our main account of this ritual is provided by a hostile Christian writer who is horrified at its gore but perhaps alarmed at its similarity of purpose as well. Perhaps he exaggerated the whole process in order to do down a religious competitor? Either way, it shows us that we have to be very careful about taking any ancient author at face value. They all have their own agendas to push and axes to grind.

It all seems so irrational. Wasn't this the world where philosophy was invented? Where Plato and Aristotle developed sophisticated arguments about the nature of knowledge, the reality of the material world, and the reasons things are as they are? How do we square the two? The simple fact is that philosophy was carried out only by a very small group of mainly upper-class men. This doesn't make their discoveries less important in the history of ideas and human intellectual development but if we want to understand the wider ancient world we have to place them in a far broader, far less educated context.

Take ancient medicine, which we tend to think of as the forerunner of modern scientific treatment. Many doctors still swear the Hippocratic oath, although they are not required to do so, in honour of the 'Father' of western medicine, Hippocrates of Cos, who lived in the fifth and fourth centuries BC. It was he, the traditional version goes, who established medicine as a stand-alone profession, based on the cool application of clinical observation. Sitting at the patient's bedside, Hippocrates applied reason to physical ailments and his case histories were written to provide others with a model in this type of inductive method. This image is, however, more a later invention than a reality. Exaggerated stories of Hippocrates' brilliant healing powers circulated after his death, which told how he cured Athens of its plague; he was even supposedly asked by the king of Persia to come and rid his lands of disease. In fact, not a single one of the roughly seventy texts in the body of works attributed to Hippocrates was definitely written by him. The oath, which may not be his work, has itself been doctored on many occasions to remove sections that no longer fit with our idea of what a physician should be. The opening line of the original, for example, makes it clear that it is the gods of healing who are being invoked: 'I swear by Apollo the Physician, Asclepius the Surgeon, and Hygeia, the god of Health and Panacea, the god of Healing ...' Religion and medicine were as intertwined as all other areas of ancient life. You could not escape the gods.

Even more surprising is that the kind of medicine practised by Hippocrates was only one approach out of many. Broadly speaking, all these doctors viewed the human body as a collection of liquids, not of organs. The body was thought to consist of four humours – black bile, yellow bile, blood, and phlegm – as well as other fluids such as sweat, semen, urine and saliva. Illness happened when these fluids got out of balance with each other. Apart from this, ancient medics don't seem to have agreed about much. They were competitors in a tough marketplace and tried to outdo each other by making their theories and treatments more attractive to potential customers than those of their rivals. Some doctors believed that there was one simple method for categorising all diseases: whether they were caused by constriction or relaxation. Others tailor-made their treatments according to the particular symptoms of the individual patient. Another approach was to try to find the underlying cause for superficial symptoms.

Ancient doctors were expensive. Most patients who visited physicians came from the top sections of society.

Everyone else looked to traditional folk remedies to treat their ailments. Pliny the Elder advises those who are suffering from a bad head cold to kiss a mule on the nose. This kind of homespun remedy is not perhaps the kind of treatment we imagine when we think of ancient medicine. Some people laughed at the pretentious theories of the doctors. In one ancient joke, a patient says to a doctor, 'I've got the runs, something must be wrong with my humours' and the doctor replies, 'You can disappear down the toilet and you won't spoil my good humour'. Magic was another widely popular means of medical diagnosis and treatment. One simple spell for a cough told the sufferer to write in black ink on hyena parchment. I'm not sure how easy it was to get hold of hyena parchment in the ancient world but I suspect this gave the cunning magician the opportunity to sell you some he already happened to have put by. Other spells were far more complicated: a cure for gout tells you to sit down and put clay under your feet, then cook an ant in henna oil, mix it with figs, raisins and potentilla, and anoint your foot with the result. Feel free to give it a try.

Sex was everywhere too. Models of grossly enlarged penises were commonly used to ward off evil spirits. Many of the images of sex might seem to us to be gay, with man-on-man action being a frequent theme. This is complicated by the fact that there was an important active/passive divide in ancient sexuality. What mattered was who was doing what to whom, not who you were having sex with. Being on top was all that counted and those on the receiving end were thought to be shameful. This was a far more status-oriented concept of sexuality than our own. It was also a way of thinking about sexuality that was not compartmentalised and cut off from everyday life, as it would be later by Christian culture. Sex and the sexual urge were considered to be a normal part of life, and representations of it were casually included in all manner of daily contexts. One grand house in Pompeii, the House of the Vettii, has a large wall painting in the entrance hall of the god Priapus weighing his penis. Fancy having an image like this in your house? Such an attitude was something later Christian writers found deeply disturbing. Prostitutes were very common in the ancient city. The cohort of young, unmarried labourers who flocked to the cities for work relied on prostitutes to meet their sexual needs. The prostitutes' work was carried out in a semi-public context, often in the many taverns, which meant that such sex acts were easily overheard. The bestial noises emanating from the brothel symbolised for the Christians what was wrong with Roman society.

Everyday language could be crude. We might think of ancient Latin and Greek as being languages of high culture, but they were also the languages of grotesque personal abuse. One graffiti claims, 'I butt-fucked Nisus ten times'. Some lead sling shots survive from the siege of Perugia by Octavian's troops in the winter of 41 BC, which the defenders fired at their attackers: 'I'm aiming for Octavian's arsehole', is scratched on one; and on another, 'Hi, Octavian: you suck dick'. Most people lived in a physical, rough-hewn world where they had to do hard manual work to make a living. It was only natural many would delight in this kind of excessive, physical insult.

High culture was a small part of the ancient world. Most

A character with the beard and giant erect phallus of Priapus from Pompeii

people were illiterate and had little or no access to the great texts that have usually been seen as epitomising the classical. Other more lowbrow texts can show us a very different side to the ancient past. Studying the ancient world today means taking completely new approaches. Archaeology can be of great help, whether it is analysing the bones of the dead in Pompeii or examining the impact of watermills. New scientific methods can help us to find out about what food people ate and what was wrong with it. Understanding an alternative past involves looking at new periods: not just classical Athens and republican Rome, but the Hellenistic kingdoms that inherited Alexander's great empire, and the late Roman empire, which we have to thank for the dominance of Christianity in the West today. Greece and Rome can no longer be seen in isolation but have to be fitted into the global history of their day. What did the Persians think of the Greeks; how does the Roman empire stack up in comparison with ancient China? And finally, understanding the ancient world lets us see how our perceptions of it have coloured our views of the modern world – from what makes good art to how we should understand Islam.

2

THE ANCIENT WORLD
FROM BELOW

How far can we approach the ancient world 'from below'? Can we begin to describe the lives of the 'ordinary' Greeks and Romans? The problem is that most of the surviving texts of classical literature pay little more than passing, and often sneering, attention to these people. But in reality this was a world where working men and social marginals such as slaves, non-citizens and women made up the great majority. Trying to recover what these voiceless people have to say means looking at a whole different set of evidence in a variety of new ways.

AN AVERAGE LIFE

Who exactly do we mean by 'ordinary' people? Well, certainly not the upper-class men who wrote most of our sources. The overwhelming majority of ancient society, somewhere between 95 to 99 per cent depending on where exactly you draw your line, was made up of the non-elite. This majority consisted of the men who earned a modest living as day labourers in the fields or doing heavy manual work on building sites in the cities. Big populations like those of Rome and Athens needed similarly large imports of all kinds of goods – from food to pots to wine – which generated a lot of work for men in carrying these goods from ship to cart to shop. It included the peasants who farmed the countless rural smallholdings and the craftsmen and small traders who supplied people with everything from shoes to knives to haircuts. The service sector consisted of a lot of street entertainers and storytellers as well as those offering solutions to people's everyday religious problems: fortune-tellers, dream-interpreters, spell-writers and astrologers. And that's just the men. The ordinary people also consisted of their wives and children. Then there were all the slaves, as well as those who had become destitute and eked out a living from scavenging and begging. 'Ordinary' turns out to refer to a great melting pot of different social groups.

Most of these people left little or no trace. They couldn't write and owned few possessions. Yet there is actually quite a lot of material that offers us a glimpse of the world and world-view of the average person. This includes fables, joke books, oracles, graffiti and visual representations of many

A shop selling meat, fruit and vegetables near Rome

kinds. The aim of this chapter is to use some of these sources to give you some idea of what life was like for these ordinary folk.

The main problem most people faced in the ancient world was economic uncertainty. They lived in a kind of shallow poverty, where they made enough money to provide a basic standard of living but never generated much more than that. This meant they had few savings or other reserves to fall back on in times of hardship. Poverty was always knocking at the door. Even middling sorts – artisans who made a reasonable income – lived under a permanent threat of impoverishment. Put simply, the man *in* the street was never far from becoming the man *on* the street.

One of the main reasons for this economic vulnerability was the unreliability of the climate. You never knew what kind of harvest you were going to get. Even today agricultural volatility can be exceptionally high in the Mediterranean basin, with annual average variations in crop yields in excess of 60 per cent in places like Tunisia. Egypt at 14 per cent has the lowest annual variation in yield by far, because of the highly regular annual flood of the Nile. It is no wonder that Roman emperors relied heavily on Egypt as well as North Africa for supplying the grain to feed Rome. By contrast, in most regions bumper harvests could easily be followed by years of dearth. Unless people had something to fall back on, the impact of these shortages could be devastating. People were most at risk if all their income came from the same source, so they tried to diversify. Farmers would plant a variety of crops so that if one failed they wouldn't be completely wiped out. (This was to be the problem during the Irish potato famine in the mid-nineteenth century. Forced onto marginal land, Catholic Irish farmers had become totally dependent on one crop. At the time Ireland as a whole was yielding good harvests in other crops, but not in potatoes.)

In ancient towns and cities, poor harvests had a knock-on effect. Food prices rose, meaning there was less money to spend on services, particularly given that food made up a large proportion of average household expenditure. Artisans, who seem to have earned more than manual labourers, could try to soften the impact of this by saving some money when work was more plentiful.

One thing it is easy for us to overlook is that small changes in income could have a significant impact on people's lives. If you have very little money and are living at or near subsistence levels then a bit less can be the difference between being adequately fed and going hungry. In economics, it is known that poor people's reported levels of happiness (and, OK, there are obvious difficulties here: what is happiness; do we believe what people say?) increase quickly for only minor additional increases in income but not beyond. In other words, people get greedy and harder to satisfy as they get better off. If you are a billionaire, then an extra one hundred million here or there makes no difference to how you feel. If you are scraping by on ten thousand, then a few hundred extra can have a major impact. A few thousand can open the door to all manner of life-enhancing expenditures, from better food and accommodation to holidays. The ancient world was no different. People tried hard to secure the kind of small-scale improvements that could significantly boost their quality of life, changes that may seem hardly worth the effort to us, but that's because we are sitting in the relative luxury of the modern world.

Another interesting aspect of the relationship between levels of happiness and income is that, once earning enough to cover a reasonable lifestyle, people find great satisfaction in being better off than others. The rich are not happy because of the absolute level of their wealth but because they are richer than everyone else. Even then, they tend to benchmark themselves against other wealthy individuals. Again, ancient society, which was acutely sensitive to minor differences in status, shows the same characteristics. Given that relatively small changes in income could have a significant effect on someone's relative standing within the community, people would naturally focus on doing everything they could to secure those small additional boosts to their income in order to rise up the social ladder.

Earning a living from day labouring or as an artisan was tough. The hard physical work ground down the body. It coarsened the hands and left bodies bent double with fatigue. Many of the ordinary people probably stank, since they lived by carrying out manual work in a hot climate. Many smelled in accordance with their trade. Tanners stank of hides, and fullers of the piss-pots that stood outside their establishments, urine being used in the processing of wool. Poor dental hygiene will have meant that many had roaring halitosis. But it was still a much better life than the fate that awaited those who fell into destitution. Some of the descriptions of these poor beggars make the skin crawl: 'their bodies are sickly', writes one Christian author, 'and they suffer from infected wounds or malignant tumours under the skin which attack their joints'. The stress that such a collapse in living standards could generate in individuals was dramatic. One astrologer says that those who suffer it become argumentative and unreasonable, with a temper that almost amounts to insanity. Those who lose everything become 'frightened, perplexed, obsessed with delusions'. Destitution was a truly terrifying experience.

Living in an ancient city took a toll on the average individual. Most people in Rome lived in tenement blocks, if, that is, their income was sufficient to pay the high rents these modest rooms cost. It's possible that many lived in shanty towns or wherever they could find shelter. The problem is that such individuals have left no record of themselves and ancient writers thought they weren't worth documenting. We just don't know how many there may have been. Those who could afford to rent lived in overcrowded conditions without cooking or heating facilities. The city offered its inhabitants greater opportunities for entertainment and employment but at a cost in comfort. Of course, overcrowding can be a subjective experience. Ordinary people may have had lower space expectations and as a result were not bothered about living in high-density housing. Again, we cannot know. Economic migrants flocked to the big cities in the hope that the streets were paved with gold. Modern evidence shows how such incomers tend to suffer from greater stress because of a variety of factors: they have weaker social support networks, without friends or family; they have often suffered traumatic experiences, either while migrating or causing migration in the first place, such as being forcibly evicted from land; they have low status and badly paid jobs; and they suffer all the problems that come with trying to integrate into a new culture.

Life for most people in ancient cities was lived in the street. They hung out in the barbershops, the fountains, marketplaces, taverns and wine-shops, and baths, all of which offered spaces for people to socialise, gossip and hear the latest news. Cato the Elder was such a killjoy that he wished the forum was paved with nothing but sharp-pointed stones to stop people lingering there. These were the public places that provided the daily sites for ordinary social activity. To a large extent, people were forced to live outside because high rents meant domestic space was at a premium. It was OK for the rich, who could afford the generous space of a villa-style house even in the urban environment. They could carry out their socialising and enjoy their entertainments in the privacy of their homes. Ordinary people had to go outside.

Taverns and wine-shops played a big part in the social life of the ancient city-dweller. Most people had no access to cooking facilities and the tavern provided a cheap and easy place to get hot food. Wine was served as well. They were so popular in Pompeii, a relatively small town with about twenty thousand inhabitants, that approximately 140 inns and bars have been found, or about one per 145 of the population, in a city that has been only half excavated. Their importance was such that the Romans had numerous names for these eating and drinking places – *taberna, popina, ganeum, caupona, hospitium, deversorium* – in the way that the Inuit are alleged to have many different words for snow. (This issue is in fact highly contentious, although the Sami of northern Scandinavia do have about 180 words for snow and ice and about a thousand for reindeer, so let's take them as a comparison.) Taverns were not just about food. In many cases they offered other diversions, including music, prostitution and gambling. They were actually frequented by all levels of society, including slaves, but often came in for condemnation by the upper classes who regarded them as overrun by commoners.

The presence of such entertainments makes it clear that living an ordinary life in an ancient city was not all death, misery and poverty. People knew how to have a good time. Whether it was watching plays in the theatre or more low-key productions put on by travelling actors in the street, going to watch the chariot-racing or just scratching a gambling-board in the ground – there is even one in the House of the Vestal Virgins (I guess they didn't have much else to do) – ordinary people had lots of ways of keeping themselves amused. The kind of thing they found funny was often very different from the more refined jokes that the educated ancients appreciated. A lot of their humour is full of farts. One very popular mime, called 'Beans', told how the new god Romulus wanted to eat beans, not the traditional food of the gods, ambrosia. Sadly, the text doesn't survive. Beans held a high place in popular Roman gastronomy, a fact borne out by the names of four of the most famous Roman families: the Lentulus family (after lentils), the Fabius (after favas), the Cicero (after chickpeas), and the Piso (after peas). And in the context of a rude play, beans meant farts – lots of them, probably. We do actually possess some surviving fart-related jokes. In one, a sailor was asked where the wind was coming from and replied, 'From the beans and onions'. It's like an ancient Carry On.

Sometimes life was just plain boring. Lots of ancient graffiti seem to have been written simply to waste a bit of time. Underemployment, due either to lack of work or the seasonality of what was available, meant that empty days were probably commonplace for many people. Scratching your name onto a wall helped fill the void. Work provided a cornerstone of non-elite identity in the way that leisure did for the elite. In simple graffiti such as 'Aufidus was here, goodbye', or the more exact 'Gaius Pumidius Dipilus was here on October 3rd', we can see people's pleasure in being able to assert their value in the face of soul-destroying inactivity. It was a kind of displacement activity for the work it temporarily replaced. Or as one graffito says, 'It took 640 paces to walk back and forth between here and there ten times'. Walking aimlessly up and down was part and parcel of everyday life for some.

Some graffiti are very polite. There are lots of simple greetings or banal 'best wishes' to friends. This basic politeness even extended to respecting other writers' scrawls, and people would make sure that they didn't write over existing text. There are about three thousand surviving graffiti in Pompeii relating to the elections that were taking place around the time Vesuvius erupted and preserved the town in ash. They tell us something about the kind of qualities that politicians thought would appeal to the average voter, who was, of course, a male citizen. Not surprisingly, politicians did not emphasise their cunning and ability to cheat. Instead they talk about themselves as being 'good', 'honest', or 'a most worthy citizen'; the candidate, it is claimed, 'lives modestly' or has 'done many things generously'. One appears to say that 'he bakes good bread'. Those that probably capture the spirit of the electorate most closely are the ones promising that the aspiring candidate 'will do something for you'. Just what the voter wants to hear. We shouldn't think that this was what Pompeian politicians were actually like, of course. Ancient politicians presented themselves in the best possible light in the same way that ours do today. But these electioneering slogans do suggest that ordinary voters wanted their representatives to be, or at least appear to be, straightforward and honest. Some tombstone inscriptions suggest that this was how people liked to think of themselves: 'modest, honest and trustworthy', says one.

But there is lots of evidence to suggest that everyday life in the ancient world wasn't always so fine or upstanding. Some graffiti suggest a society rife with crime: 'A copper pot went missing from my shop. Anyone who returns it to me will be given 65 sestertii. 20 more will be given for information leading to the capture of the thief.' Stealing was a recurrent problem. In Roman Bath, for example, over a hundred lead curse tablets were recovered from the waters of the spring, nearly all of them appeals for divine retribution by victims of theft. One person who had had six silver coins stolen dedicates them to the goddess of the baths, Sulis Minerva. Now it is the criminal who has a problem because he or she has stolen the money from a god, not just any old human. As the curse says, 'It is for the goddess to exact the coins back from them'. Some of the demands for punishment seem way out of line with the severity of the crime committed. One demands that the thief who has stolen a pair of gloves should 'go mad and lose their eyes in the goddess's temple'. An eye for a glove is pretty rough justice.

Ordinary people often seem to have lived lives dominated by fear and riven with animosity. We can get a sense of this in the many proverbs that survive. Most of these texts dealt with the most important issues of life: birth, marriage, children, death, dealing with superiors. 'Life is uncertain for a poor man when a greedy rich man lives nearby', warns one. Pithy and memorable, they provided a practical problem-solving toolkit for the average person to help solve the challenges they would face in their daily lives. One proverb is optimistic about the benefits of not having much money: 'Poverty is the sister to good sense', it claims. Many are far less positive about how other people will behave towards you. One example is extremely hostile to women, warning 'Don't trust a woman till she's dead'. People liked these proverbs because they were traditional and respected. They also liked new sayings, which neatly encapsulated everyday problems. Their popularity can be gauged from the fact that good sayings could generate a round of applause when they appeared in plays in the theatres.

Fables provide a similar picture of a world driven by anxiety. They are full of wild beasts. In Aesop's famous fables, for example, we find thirty-seven lions and twenty-nine wolves. These were the kinds of animal that loomed terrifyingly large in the popular imagination. We can see them as personifying the dangers people faced in forms that could be easily understood. These animals represent a world of threat and competition, where danger lurks behind every corner, and only the most vigilant can hope to survive. It's a world where poverty and destitution are only ever a stone's throw away, but also a world where huge social and economic inequality is seen as perfectly natural. It's a world where nothing much changes, where the same forces and characters dominate. The size of the economic pie never grows, meaning no one gets richer unless it is at another's expense. There is a limited amount of 'good' to go round, so the best you could hope for was to hang on to what little you had in the face of strong competition from others.

WHAT WERE ORDINARY PEOPLE LIKE?

What kind of person thrived in the ancient world? Or, to put it another way, what kind of personalities did ordinary people have in antiquity? One Aesop fable describes how Eros was born the child of Poverty and Resourcefulness. He inherited the characteristics of both of his parents. Like his mother, Poverty, he was badly dressed, had no shoes and slept rough. Like his father, he was bold, cunning and street-wise. Perhaps these were the kind of personal characteristics any normal person had to have if they wanted to survive in the rough and tumble of ordinary life in the ancient world. We certainly find a lot of this toughness in ancient graffiti. Much of it employs an aggressive, mocking but jocular tone towards its readers and interlocutors, treating them as semi-serious rivals in a textual-verbal competition. It is a type of social interaction we would call 'banter'. For example, a prayer on a wall in Pompeii's basilica began as follows, 'Agatho, the slave of Herennius, asks Venus ...' but then halted mid-sentence, before being finished by another hand who supplied the end as, 'I ask that I die'. Not clever and not that funny but typical of the spirit of joking rivalry pervading much graffiti. Often there was an element of macho, sexual bragging about these taunts: 'Floronius, privileged soldier of the 7th legion, was here. The women did not know of his presence. Only six women came to know, too few for such a stallion.' Another advised that, 'If anyone does not believe in Venus, they should gaze at my girlfriend'. Or they denigrated the sexuality of others: 'Amplicatus, I know that Icarus is buggering you. Salvius wrote this.'

Some of it was pretty crude. 'Theophilus, don't perform oral sex on girls against the city wall like a dog', advises one graffito on a street wall. Some of it was plain abusive: 'Epaphra, you are bald!' said one; another, 'Chie, I hope your haemorrhoids rub together so much that they hurt worse than they ever have before!' This focus on bums and so on was widespread: 'Innkeeper, I have wet the bed. I know I've done wrong. If you want to know why, it was because there was no chamber pot.' Another simply stated that, 'Secundus shat here'. Women were a common target of such banter. In the Tavern of Verecundus, Restitutus wrote, 'Restituta, take off your tunic, please, and show us your hairy privates'.

We find the same kind of competitive, macho banter in other areas of ordinary life too. One board has the spaces arranged into letters to provide a gaming table, which then form words that insult the person playing the game:

LEVATE	DALOCU
LUDERE	NESCIS
IDIOTA	RECEDE

Get up from your place
You don't know how to play
Get lost you idiot

Clement of Alexandria criticises men in bars who aimed their banter at passing women and even swore at people for a laugh. Whether these targets perceived the banter as good humour or simple abuse is impossible to say.

From the male point of view, banter served some positive functions. This kind of jocular sparring helped to create a sense of male community, a kind of male bonding, in the same way that it can in the pub today. It was not purely designed to wound the recipient and the shared humour it generated boosted group morale. Abusing a member of the group by calling him names can also be seen as a way of emphasising the supremacy of the collective over the individual. However competitive their world, ordinary working people needed each other to survive, whether it was working together in a fishing boat or a building site, or serving in the legions. There was no room for the individual to be sensitive about such personal attacks. The average man was expected to be tough enough to laugh off taunts and share in the communal laughter. Nonetheless, this was a type of social interaction that was patently aggressive and argumentative.

It's easy to think of people as being gullible or even stupid for believing in so many strange and ridiculous things, like magic and divination. Yet people don't seem to have been as simple as is sometimes suggested. In fact, a healthy dose of scepticism was needed if you weren't going to be taken for a ride. In one Greek joke, an astrologer casts the horoscope of a sick boy, promises his mother he will live a long time, and then demands his fee. She says she will give it to him tomorrow. 'But what happens if he dies in the night?' replies the astrologer. And there's the one where someone on a trip asks a charlatan prophet how his family are back home. Being told they are all well, especially his father, he says, 'But my father's been dead for years!' 'Ah,' the prophet replies, 'clearly you do not know who your real father is!' People were too streetwise to be easily conned. Just because they believed in a wide variety of supernatural forces didn't mean that they weren't sceptical about individual practitioners. Nor did an occasional charlatan shake their belief in how the supernatural worked, in the same way that seeing a bad doctor today wouldn't make you lose faith in modern medicine as a whole.

You find the same combination of shared struggle in many of the graffiti that were written about women. In some the male lover calls for unity among all lovers: 'Whoever loves, let him flourish. Let him die who doesn't know love. Let him die twice over whoever forbids love.' The male is established as a weak figure in the face of feminine power: 'Why do you put off our joy and kindle hope and tell me always to come back tomorrow. So, force me to die since you force me to live without you. Your gift will be to stop torturing me.' This is how men liked to see and portray themselves, emphasising their powerlessness in the face of passion. It was also designed to show that their passion was as great as their manliness. Only a real man could feel this strongly and only a real man could ever hope to overcome his rivals and win the woman as his prize. It's a macho view of the world. In reality we can see this kind of group self-mockery as being designed to conceal the imbalance that existed in gender relations. Another piece of graffiti says, 'Take hold of your servant girl whenever you want to; it's your right.' Women were at risk from predatory males: 'May Love burn in some lonely mountains whoever wants to rape my girlfriend.' Regrettably, we do not know what ordinary women thought about this kind of banter.

But ancient sexuality was driven by different ideas of what was acceptable. When a piece of graffiti claims, 'Weep, you girls. My penis has given you up. Now it penetrates men's bums. Goodbye, wondrous femininity!', we shouldn't interpret it as an example of a repressed gay man coming out, or as another piece of male banter. It was perfectly normal for men to want to penetrate any others they found attractive, whether they were women, men, girls or boys. As we have seen, the only important criterion was whether the man was taking the active part in the sex. Being a man meant being on top in every sense.

Marriage was almost universal. A girl probably had some say in choosing a husband but if her father wanted the marriage to take place there would be little she could do to resist it. What would it have been like to be, for example, a fourteen-year-old girl being taken to her new thirty-year-old husband's house? There is a story of a young bride being eaten by the household guard dog when she tried to run away on her wedding night because she was so terrified of having sex for the first time. In another text, we hear of a virgin girl whose young husband quickly forced himself on her and afterwards earned from her 'the kind of terrified hate that follows unnatural force'. The concept of rape inside marriage was not something any Roman man would have recognised.

Wives were expected to obey their husbands. Domestic violence was probably common. St Augustine describes how many women were beaten by their husbands and bore the scars on their faces. When they complained to Augustine's mother, she simply said that they should think of their wedding certificates as the documents that had turned them into slaves; and like slaves they should not be insolent towards their masters. In dream interpretation, it was considered bad to dream of beating your wife, not because of the violence itself but because the dream meant she was having an affair. In other words, assault would have been considered a natural response on the husband's part if he found out that his wife was cheating. Most women were probably sufficiently cowed that they suffered the blows in silence. One astrologer predicted that girls born under a certain alignment of the stars would be like those wives who are subject to all kinds of injuries from their husbands but have such a gentle character that they would patiently bear these injuries all their lives.

Women were expected to behave in bed as well. As the Greek dream-interpreter Artemidorus explains, if a man dreams he has sexual intercourse with his wife and she yields willingly, submissively, and without reluctance then it is good for everyone. It's not surprising that women living in this kind of domestic environment seem to have repressed their true feelings. One Roman writer – a man, obviously – emphasises that wives should have no emotions of their own, but should imitate whatever mood the husband happens to be in. If he's happy she should laugh with him, but if he is miserable she too should be serious. It was perfectly acceptable for men to have sex with certain other women, such as prostitutes. Slave owners in particular seem to have taken advantage of any of their slaves – their possessions – that they fancied. We have no idea how the wives felt about this. Did they, like their husbands, perceive such behaviour as harmless? Most wives were not in a position to complain even if they objected. St Augustine tells how his mother served her husband as if he were her master, and put up with his sexual infidelities with such patience that she never even complained about them.

Women were expected to control their emotions in public, and probably in private too. In a way we can see this as training for the emotional roles they would have to fulfil in their adult lives. Sometimes they had to be meek and submissive, at other times, such as at funerals or when pleading with enemies, they were expected to produce dramatic emotional outbursts. Grief was a core part of a woman's work. After the death of her husband, she was required to enter into a long period of ritualised mourning, lasting well after the funeral. Only a generous display of grief could accurately reflect the importance of the dead man who had been the source of the woman's identity in the first place.

In reality, women were not only symbolically reliant on their men. In most families it was the man who was the main breadwinner, which left a woman exceptionally vulnerable if he died. Widowhood was synonymous with extreme poverty. Many widows had to try to reduce the number of mouths they were left to feed. In one papyrus letter, a women tries to persuade another family to adopt her child: 'My husband died and I was left to toil and suffer for my daughter by him … and now I no longer have the means to feed her. I have requested that you receive her from me as your daughter.' Harsh, but the best way to offer both mother and daughter some security.

Children were expensive and the head of the family had to make sure there were never too many mouths to feed. Contraception was limited to the rhythm method and some herbal potions that will have had little or no effect. Throwing unwanted babies away, a practice known as 'exposure', served as a perfectly acceptable form of post-partum birth control. In Egypt, at about the time of the birth of Jesus, one absent father, Hilarion, wrote to his expectant wife: 'If you have the baby before I return, let it live if it is a boy; if it is a girl, expose it.' Exposure horrifies us but the ancients had no such qualms. It gave the infant a chance of survival because abandoned babies could be picked up by those unable to have children, those whose own children had died, those looking for foundlings to bring up as slaves, and slave dealers looking for babies to rear for a few years – they would use wet nurses to start with – before selling them on. Many of the exposed babies will, however, have died from the cold or, as one source describes, have been eaten by dogs.

Women had to cope with the natural deaths of their

children. The average woman in this period saw two or three die (or be thrown away by their fathers). How did women feel about this? Obviously, we know that losing a child is one of the worst things imaginable for a parent. Does that mean that women were often paralysed with grief for those that had died and with fear for those that still lived? Or did they limit their emotional attachment to babies until they had passed the critical early stage and were therefore much more likely to survive? You find this kind of strategy at work in some modern Third World slums. There is a hint of it at work in a Roman legal document, which states that children over six years of age can be mourned for a year, but children under six only for a month. On the other hand, Seneca talks of a mother pitying a beggar because she wonders whether he could be the son who she exposed as a baby, which suggests something other than a simple throwaway mentality. Some seem to have been as anguished as any mother would be today when one of her children is seriously ill. An Egyptian woman called Isidora wrote to her brother and husband – incest was a common Egyptian practice – begging him to come home to his sick child. The mother's anguish is revealed in the change in syntax and the staccato phrases: 'Do anything, postpone everything, and come, preferably tomorrow. The baby is ill. It has become thin. It is already 200 days since you went away. I fear it will die in your absence. Know for sure: if it dies in your absence, be prepared to find me hanged.'

How fathers felt is hard to tell. They were expected to be able to take tough decisions, even about whether their children should live, suggesting that they were better able to cope with infant mortality. One strategy was to use black humour as a way of distancing death. In one Greek joke, a blockhead who has just buried his son happens to meet the boy's teacher: 'I'm sorry my son was absent from school', he apologises; 'You see, he is dead.' (I sometimes tell this one to students to show how ideas of what's funny change over time. It never gets a laugh.)

The ancient attitude to children was far less sentimental than our own. Children were an expensive investment, a kind of pension for the parents for their old age. Most could not afford to educate their offspring and needed to get them out to work at a young age. One gravestone, set

A midwife assisting at a birth

up for a nine-year-old called Viccentia ('a very nice girl', it says), describes her as a gold-worker. Beatings seem to have been routine. Sexual abuse of slave girls and boys was probably widespread and certainly not seen as strange. Perhaps the most extreme example of physical child abuse is Seneca's description of men who make a living raising exposed infants and mutilating them before sending them out to beg, which at least suggests that some Romans took pity and gave them money.

Childbirth was exceptionally dangerous to the mother in the ancient world. This meant that stepmothers were frequently found bringing up the children of their husband's dead wife. Some, like Cinderella's, were infamous for the harsh treatment they handed out to these inherited children. As one text says, a stepmother 'would never love her stepchild by inclination or choice'. They were assumed to be giving most of the food to their own children and starving the stepchildren.

The ancient world was full of death, but most ordinary people seem to have given more thought to the problems of the here-and-now than to the afterlife. There was no general belief that the gods would reward human good behaviour in the future. Ideas about the afterlife did exist, though. Some of the messages on tombstones are resolutely miserable: the phrase 'I was not, I was, I am not, I don't care' (in Latin *non fui, fui, non sum, non curo*) was so common it was often abbreviated to simply nffnsnc. An end to the back-breaking toil of everyday life is a common theme. As one woman's tombstone says, 'Where have you gone, dear soul, seeking rest from troubles, For what else but trouble did you have all your life?' Life in the ancient world was hard for most people. They were largely untouched by the high culture we associate with the classical past. But if we widen our scope, we can still pick up some glimpses of these hidden individuals.

3

WHAT, WHEN AND WHERE
IS THE ANCIENT WORLD?

What do you study when you learn about the ancient world? Ask most people and they will say it is Greece and Rome. And until a generation ago many courses focused not just on Greece and Rome but specifically on classical Athens and republican Rome. These were the periods when the artistic, intellectual and military achievements of the ancients were perceived to be at their height. In Athens, Aeschylus, Sophocles and Euripides were writing their great plays, Aristophanes was putting on his comedies, and Socrates was annoying everyone with his nit-picking and endless questioning. In Rome, the happy relationship between the Senate and the Roman people saw them conquer vast tracts of the Mediterranean world and start to produce their own great literature in conscious imitation of the Greeks. All of which is true. But in the same way in which the study of the ancient world has expanded to include all sections of society, so has it spread through space and time to cover the many other cultures and periods that surrounded these two 'classical' periods, narrowly defined. What I want to do in this chapter is to give you a flavour of some of this diversity, and a sense of the importance of other periods in the ancient world. I'm going to begin by looking at the

Hellenistic world, which developed after the break-up of Alexander the Great's kingdom following his death. Then I'm going to show how it is the late Roman empire, forever tainted by Gibbon's account of its decline and fall, that we have to thank for many of the ancient influences on the modern world.

ALEXANDER AND THE HELLENISTIC WORLD

First Alexander. When he died in 323 BC, Alexander had conquered as far as the Indus, the Oxus and the Nile. Vast territories came under Greek control. Even though his death meant that Alexander's empire soon split apart, the kingdoms that replaced it were ruled by a Greek ruling class. Most famous of these were the Ptolemies in Egypt, the last of whom was Cleopatra some three centuries later. Greek culture, traders and colonists flowed into these regions, mingling with the indigenous cultures to create a series of vibrant fusions. Traditionally dismissed as a period of decline, the Hellenistic period offers a rich supply of evidence for the emergence of a new kind of ancient Greek world.

One of the reasons why the post-Alexander era was seen as a comedown from Alexander's brief rule was, well, it was after Alexander. His military achievements had been so brilliant that when he died the generals and friends who scrapped over his empire seemed a pretty mediocre bunch by comparison. Alexander had left no official heir and different parts of his army supported different candidates.

The infantry wanted his half-brother, Arrhidaeus, while the cavalry supported their leader Perdiccas's position of waiting to see if Alexander's unborn child by his wife Roxana turned out to be a boy. Perdiccas won out and in an agreement in Babylon in 323 BC he carved up the empire among his various supporters. After various squabbles, Alexander's empire settled down into four separate kingdoms: the Antigonids in Greece; the Ptolemies in Egypt; the Seleucids in Syria, Mesopotamia and Persia; and the Attalids in the area around Pergamum in modern Turkey. The most easterly area, centred on what is today Afghanistan, was nominally a part of the Seleucid empire, but distance meant that the Greek rulers were effectively autonomous. It was all a good bit less glorious than Alexander's eleven-year blitzkrieg across the Near East.

But even though Alexander had been a great empire-winner he was not a great empire-builder. Addicted to conquest, he was less interested in the nitty-gritty of establishing the kind of efficient administration which might have unified his empire and seen it survive. Of course he might have managed to consolidate his territories if he had lived longer. As it happened, it was left

Alexander the Great

to his various successors to get a grip on their new kingdoms and establish their rule on a sound footing.

Alexander loved founding cities. His ancient biographer Plutarch says that he built at least seventy, although many of these foundations probably consisted of rebranding pre-existing settlements. He certainly started at least twenty from scratch, most of which he modestly named after himself. Cities called Alexandria cropped up as far apart as Alexandria in Egypt to Alexandria the Furthest in central Asia, today's Tajikistan. It was these cities that became the focus of the spread of Greek culture into Asia. Built on a grid-plan like a modern American city, they had all the facilities you would have expected to find in a traditional town in mainland Greece: a theatre, gymnasium, and houses with colonnades and courtyards. Enticed by the opportunities these towns offered new settlers, many Greeks left the crowded lands of their own country and headed east to seek their fortunes. The cities of old Greece that had once been pre-eminent, cities such as Athens and Sparta, were now overshadowed by the glitzy new streets of Alexandria in Egypt and Antioch in Syria, the capitals of the Ptolemaic and Seleucid kingdoms.

And with Greek colonists came Greek ideas. The library in the Egyptian Alexandria housed hundreds of thousands of ancient scrolls. Building on the principles of logical argument developed by Greeks in the earlier classical period, scholars based across the Hellenistic world came up with a range of new theories and discoveries. The medic Herophilos was the first doctor to dissect the human body and describe the nervous system. Euclid's system of geometry

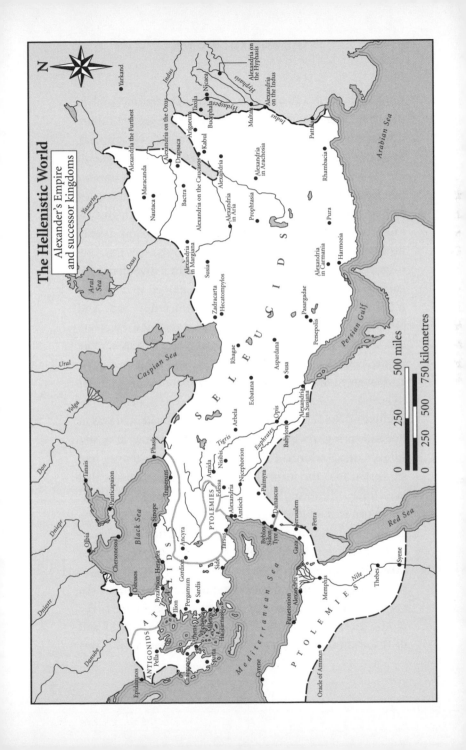

The Hellenistic World

Alexander's Empire and successor kingdoms

N

Yarkand

Indus

Alexandria on the Hyphasis

Nicaea

Hyphasis

Hydaspes

Taxila

Alexandria on the Indus

Arigaeum

Bucephala

Multan

Alexandria the Furthest

Alexandria on the Oxus

Drapsaca

Kabul

Indus

Pattala

Arabian Sea

Maracanda

Bactra

Alexandria on the Caucasus

Alexandria

Alexandria in Arachosia

Rhambacia

Nautaca

Alexandria in Aria

Prophtasia

Pura

Yaxartes

Alexandria in Margiana

Harmozia

Aral Sea

Susia

Alexandria in Carmania

Oxus

Zadracarta

Hecatompylos

Pasargadae

Persepolis

Ural

Rhagae

S E L E U C I D S

Persian Gulf

Caspian Sea

Aspardana

Susa

Ecbatana

Alexandria in Susiana

500 miles

Volga

Arbela

Opis

250

500

Tigris

Babylon

750 kilometres

Don

Phasis

Amida

Nisibis

Nicephorion

Euphrates

250

500

Palmyra

Tanais

Trapezunt

P T O L E M I E S

Edessa

Panticapaion

Sinope

Alexandria

Damascus

Olbia

Ancyra

Antioch

Jerusalem

Chersonesos

Byzantion

Heraclea

Tarsus

Petra

Red Sea

Odessos

Gordion

Side

Byblos

Sidon

Tyre

Gaza

A T T A L I D S

Pergamum

Sardis

Syene

Tilion

Dniepr

Pella

Ilion

Halicarnassos

Mediterranean Sea

Memphis

Nile

Thebes

Epidamnos

ANTIGONIDS

Athens

Sparta

Chaeronea

Paraetonion

Alexandria

P T O L E M I E S

Dniestr

Danube

Cyrene

Oracle of Ammon

Black Sea

0

remained dominant until the nineteenth century; and in maths he provided the first proof that there are an infinite number of prime numbers (please don't ask me what it was). Eratosthenes, the Head Librarian at Alexandria, used geometry to calculate the size of the earth and probably how far it is from the sun. His calculation came up with an answer of 252,000 stades for the circumference of the earth (yes, he knew it was round). Unfortunately, we don't know exactly how long his stade was. Various ancient sources give slightly different lengths, but even allowing for this divergence his calculation was somewhere between 24,500 and 28,000 miles when the real figure is 24,902, which ain't bad. And just to prove that this wasn't a fluke, he managed to calculate the tilt of the earth's axis to within one degree. Oh, and he worked out that a year should be 365 and a quarter days, and invented the idea of a leap day every four years in order to keep the calendar in line with the seasons. Later, in first-century BC Rome, when an inaccurate lunar calendar was in use and spring was bursting out in the mid-winter months, Julius Caesar reformed the calendar as Eratosthenes had suggested into the form that is basically the same as that used today. Mind you, his contemporaries thought that Eratosthenes was a bit of a jack-of-all-trades because he was always studying many different things. They called him 'Beta' which means something like 'Second-rate' or 'First Loser'.

Perhaps the most impressive physical example of the sophistication of Hellenistic scientific achievement is the Antikythera mechanism. This dates from the second half of the second century BC and is so called because it was recovered from an ancient shipwreck off the Greek island of Antikythera. This extraordinary device is nothing less than a mechanical analogue computer and is the most sophisticated mechanism known from the ancient world. Using at least thirty bronze gears, it can predict, among other things, when both lunar and solar eclipses will happen. It is phenomenally complicated. The upper back dial, for example, and to quote the team dedicated to this project, 'is in the form of a spiral, with 47 divisions per turn, displaying the 235 months of the 19-year Metonic cycle. This dial contains a smaller subsidiary dial which displays the 76-year Callippic cycle' (again, please don't ask). The Hellenistic age produced other artefacts besides those of scientific excellence. Two of the most famous Greek sculptures, the Laocoön in the Vatican Museum and the Venus de Milo in the Louvre, both date from this period.

Of course, Greek settlers did not travel with the aim of spreading Greek culture. They wanted to benefit from access to land, from making money in trade and from having positions of power in the new Greek administrations. The Greek language became the language of government and enabled a small cultural minority to retain a hold on power. But the flow of culture was not only one-way. In areas such as religion, new forms of deity were added to the list of those popular with the Greeks. The Egyptian goddess Isis, for example, became widely worshipped.

Alexander himself had been in favour of this kind of cultural fusion. He had attempted to merge the ruling classes of both the Greeks and the Persians by encouraging them to intermarry. He appointed Persians as well as

Greeks to positions of power. He married two non-Greek women: Roxana, who was a Bactrian – like the camels, she was from central Asia – and Stateira, who was the daughter of the defeated Persian King, Darius. He started to dress like a Persian, as well as taking on some of the court ceremonies and attendants that traditionally surrounded the Persian kings. Most shockingly for the Greeks, Alexander insisted that all those who appeared before him, whether Greek or Persian, should prostrate themselves. Full-length on-the-ground submission was something that the Greeks only ever carried out before the gods and for Alexander to demand it was seen as an act of supreme arrogance.

Whether Alexander was really into cultural fusion is unclear. It may have been a policy designed to fuse the two ruling elites because he realised that a small group of Greeks could never hope to hold down such a large empire on their own. Perhaps he was actually trying to turn the Persians into something close to the Greeks by creating a hybrid culture that drew elements from both. His marriage to a Persian princess was clearly aimed at establishing a royal dynasty that both sides could buy into. Or was it all just a short-term measure designed to keep the lid on the empire? His army was small and his decision to add Persian troops to it can be seen as simply a response to a chronic shortage of manpower. Alexander needed the support and loyalty of the local leaders he had conquered. Representing himself as a man with a foot in both camps, Alexander probably wanted to soften the edges of his Greekness and make it more palatable to his new subjects. They were less likely to rebel if they thought he was, if not one of them, at least able to understand their traditions and concerns. That said, Alexander also had the idea of completely unifying the cultures of Europe and Asia in a Stalinesque programme of mass migration and resettlement. So perhaps all his acts in the field of multiculturalism should be seen in the light of his paranoia at sitting on top of a great empire with only a tiny force of Greeks to protect him.

Alexander's successors were also forced to adapt themselves to local traditions and adopt many of their practices out of a need to maintain control. One example of this is in Egypt, where the Ptolemies turned themselves into something like the Pharaohs, portraying themselves as god-kings. The locals expected their rulers to be gods, or as near as dammit, and their new Greek overlords did not want to disappoint them. Presenting themselves as divine was a simple way to reinforce their hold on power. This was something of a change from how the Greeks had usually seen their leaders. Kings were traditionally regarded as tyrants, whose religious propaganda was to be recognised as such.

This uncomfortable reality meant that the Hellenistic era saw a change in traditional Greek politics. Mainland Greek cities, such as Athens, had already had to accept the rule of a king when Alexander's father, Philip, had subdued them. Now Greeks were seeing their rulers portraying themselves as gods. It all called for a new kind of political theory. It was argued that having an ideal king was in fact the best form of rule. Democracy of the type in Athens had proved to be too unstable. In democracy, it was the people who behaved like a tyrant, acting in a volatile and aggressive manner to other states and forcing the rich in their own society to spend vast sums on public benefits. An ideal king, by contrast, could be expected to rule rationally and in everyone's best interests. In this way he was himself something of a hybrid between Greek rationalism and Persian monarchy. He was a king who deserved to be king on merit and because of his own personal qualities. Indeed the benefit of absolute power was that it allowed these qualities to be clearly expressed. Rather than an arbitrary tyrant surrounded by sycophants, the ideal king was advised by a group of close companions and friends who were in a position to speak truth unto power. The divine wrapping – the grand clothes and other symbols of power – were all there simply to establish authority and reflect the ideal king's right to be on the throne. This benevolent dictatorship provided the benefits of rational leadership to the Persians and the advantages of political stability to the Greeks.

We can recognise and see through such rationalisations. Swapping the radical democracy of classical Athens for a world where autocracy was sugar-coated by political theory went down badly in the later western world, and is one reason why the Hellenistic age used to be perceived as one of decline. There may have been some anti-eastern bias at work here, too. The Greeks sometimes looked down on the Persians and could be snobbish about Alexander adopting barbarian practices. Likewise, in the nineteenth century, when the European powers had their own empires, the eastern Ottoman and Chinese empires were seen as decadent and decrepit, objects of disdain rather than admiration. The very word Hellenistic is a Victorian term, and suggests that such worth as the period does have derives from its inherent colonialism: that it was the inflow of Greek ideas to the East that makes it interesting, not the other way round. If we're not careful, we can fall into the trap of seeing everything good as coming from the Greeks, everything corrupting from the Persians. Instead, we should see it as a period where immigration created fusions and frictions between different cultural groups, an age of creativity that needed compromise on both sides to succeed.

THE LATE ROMAN EMPIRE

The history of Rome has a period that is comparable to the Hellenistic age. When we think of the Roman empire, images of the empire of the first century AD spring to mind: huge public buildings like the Colosseum, emperors ranging from the idealised first emperor Augustus to the mad excesses of Nero and Caligula. It was the second century that Gibbon characterised as the most happy and prosperous in all human history. This was the period when the empire faced few significant external threats, when the arts flourished, and instead of the likes of Nero a series of good emperors reigned, men who were selected on merit and carried out their jobs conscientiously.

From then on it starts to look bad. The peace was shattered in the third century when the empire faced a series of invasions from a number of Germanic tribes at the same time as it was confronted by a reinvigorated Persian empire in the east. The combined threat was too much for the military. It was also too much for one man to cope with. The emperor could not be in all the trouble spots at once, with the result that lots of other claimants to the throne tried to fill the power vacuum. Civil wars resulted as rival emperors sought to achieve dominance. There were twenty-seven emperors in the 266-year period from when Augustus first reigned until 235 AD, the year from which the crisis is usually dated. In other words, emperors lasted an average of ten years. In the next fifty years, there were twenty-six official emperors (in that they were recognised by the Senate) and twenty-five would-be emperors. That is to say, a new emperor came along every two years, or every year if you count them all. The empire fragmented under the pressure. Three separate zones existed side by side: the empire proper, the Gallic empire in the north, and the Palmyrene empire under Queen Zenobia in the east. For a while it looked like the days of the Roman empire were numbered.

But then came Diocletian. When he was first proclaimed emperor by his troops in 284 AD you wouldn't have given him much more chance of surviving than the many hapless emperors who had come before him. But Diocletian was made of different stuff. For one thing he was a realist. He understood that the Roman empire was no longer fit for purpose. He therefore brought in a series of reforms that transformed the Roman state.

First, the military. The Roman army had been exposed by the previous multiple invasions. Diocletian increased its size from about four hundred thousand to around five hundred and fifty or six hundred thousand. He upgraded the defences along the borders and distinguished between the lower-grade troops who manned these defences and

those who formed a new mobile field army in reserve. It was this crack force, expanded much further by Diocletian's successors, which had the flexibility to go wherever the threat existed. When the invaders had broken through the frontier region during the crisis period, they had been free to roam and ransack as they pleased. Now they would quickly be confronted by a powerful force of Rome's best soldiers.

The Emperor Diocletian

But an army cost. Increasing its size meant raising taxes to pay for it. The Roman empire was relatively lightly taxed, particularly by our standards. Most modern western governments account for about 40 to 50 per cent of total economic output, as measured by Gross Domestic Product. In the ancient world, this figure was more like 5 to 6 per cent. The ancient state had no interest in providing health care, education, or widespread social security benefits. It existed to maintain order within and keep enemies without. About two thirds of government outlays went on the army. The knock-on effect for ordinary taxpayers of Diocletian's reform was substantial. Raising government expenditure by 2 to 3 per cent of GDP seems tiny to us but in a world where small differences in income could have a major impact on the quality of life, the effect was significant. The state itself would have to be changed if people were to be compelled to hand over these substantial new taxes.

So Diocletian established a far more powerful state in order to extract a much larger tax take from the empire's inhabitants. Bureaucracy ballooned. Instead of the original 42 provinces, there were now about 120, grouped into 12 under an official called a vicar. The management became more professional, with civil governors being forced to leave their military commands to focus on raising taxes. The command of the army was left in the hands of military professionals. With bigger bureaucracy came more red tape. The central civil service kept detailed records in duplicate, had its own flowery style of writing called 'heavenly letters', created dozens of new technical terms for administrative procedures, and charged fees for their services. One civil servant earned a salary of only nine gold coins for his first year as a junior official but earned a thousand from the fees he charged for providing people with access to the government's services. Whether this amounted to corruption is hard to say. It kept the costs down for the government and transferred them onto the users. It also served to restrict access to government to those who could afford it.

Diocletian wasted no time in Rome. He realised that he needed to be where the action was. The second-century emperor Antoninus Pius didn't leave Italy once during his long reign; Diocletian probably only visited Rome once during his. Now Rome was where the emperor was. Wanting to be close to where he might be needed, Diocletian chose to spend most of his time in Nicomedia in what is now mainland Turkey. Here he built suitably grand buildings and established his court. The style of this court was completely different to that of the first emperor, Augustus. Just as the

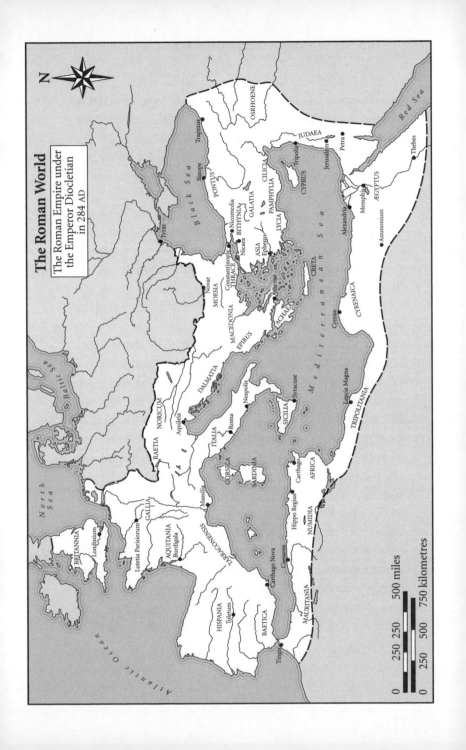

The Roman World

The Roman Empire under the Emperor Diocletian in 284 AD

N

Red Sea

OSRHOENE

JUDAEA

Trapezus

Sinope

PONTUS

Nicomedia

BITHYNIA

Nicaea

GALATIA

CILICIA

PAMPHYLIA

LYCIA

CYPRUS

Tripolis

Jerusalem

Petra

Thebes

Black Sea

ASIA

Ephesus

Constantinople

THRACE

Athenae

CRETA

Alexandria

Memphis

AEGYPTUS

Ammonium

Novae

MOESIA

MACEDONIA

EPIRUS

ACHAEA

CYRENAICA

Cyrene

Mediterranean Sea

Baltic Sea

Tyras

DALMATIA

NORICUM

RAETIA

Aquileia

ITALIA

Neapolis

Roma

SICILIA

Syracuse

Lepcis Magna

TRIPOLITANIA

North Sea

BRITANNIA

Londinium

GALLIA

Lutetia Parisiorum

AQUITANIA

Burdigala

Massilia

CORSICA

SARDINIA

Carthago

AFRICA

Hippo Regius

NUMIDIA

TARRACONENSIS

HISPANIA

Toletum

BAETICA

Carthago Nova

Caesarea

MAURITANIA

Tingis

Atlantic Ocean

0   250 250   500 miles

0   250   500   750 kilometres

Roman government had become tougher, so too the image of the emperor became fiercer. Instead of being styled 'First citizen', people now had to call Diocletian 'Dominus' (Lord or Master), the same word a slave had to call his owner. The emperor started to look like an eastern despot, dressed in a full purple cloak and a bejewelled diadem on his head, a god-like figure before whom people had to prostrate themselves. Surrounded by courtiers and eunuchs – they could be trusted because they couldn't have children who they might try to put on the throne – the emperor now sat like a colossus at the top of a great government. Scary and intimidating: who wouldn't pay their taxes, however big the demand?

For all his power, Diocletian was faced by an economy in trouble. In the crisis period, emperors had simply minted new coins in base metal to pay their soldiers as and when needed, which was often. The silver content of the denarius had fallen from 95 per cent in the early empire to less than 5 per cent. The result was hyperinflation. It's very unclear as to the extent and speed with which this happened, but the price of wheat, the basic commodity, rose about one hundred-fold in the third century. Diocletian's response was to issue his Edict on Maximum Prices, which limited the price of hundreds of goods and services, from the cost of fish and Chinese silk to the price of slaves and a haircut. It's easy for us to scoff at the naivety of this Canute-like attempt to stop prices rising. Yet only a century ago people had little idea about how inflation happened. It made sense to an ancient leader to blame rising prices on greedy traders and suppliers.

Diocletian effectively turned the Roman empire into an army camp. The value of citizenship, already devalued since it had been extended to all free men by Caracalla in 212 AD, fell to new lows. The creation of new super-elites in the bureaucracy and army, who drew their power from their proximity to the emperor, meant that the little people got forgotten. Roman law now meted out harsher punishments to those who were from more humble backgrounds. Free-born peasants were now forced to stay on the land where they were registered. They and their families became like serfs, tied to their land in perpetuity to ensure a steady flow of taxes into the treasury's coffers and conscripts into the army. Minority groups, such as the Christians, were systematically persecuted.

Diocletian established a pan-European superstate. He was so successful that he managed to retire to another of his palaces, in Split, in modern Croatia, where he allegedly spent his days growing cabbages. That he managed to retire is a sign of how successful he had been in re-establishing peace and order. But it was short-lived. He had tried to create a system where power was shared among a small group of generals, known as the Tetrarchy. Emperors would in theory now simply be promoted to the position according to their merits. The system had the advantage that, for a while, it converted potential rivals into colleagues. But it could not cope with the problems of succession and after Diocletian's death the Tetrarchy fell apart, resulting in another civil war. The ultimate successor was a man who would build on Diocletian's reforms and change the world forever. His name was Constantine.

Constantine had a vision. Literally. Before the Battle of the Milvian Bridge, which cemented his position as ruler of the western half of the empire, he saw a cross of light above the sun along with the words 'With this sign you will conquer'. As a result, he converted to Christianity. We think of conversion as being an all-or-nothing event. You can't say that you're a Christian who believes Muhammad to be the true prophet. The ancient world was different. The overwhelming majority of the population were still pagan at the time Constantine converted. They were used to employing a variety of religious practices according to what best suited their needs. The fact that the emperor was now openly following Christianity did not mean that most people understood this new faith to be incompatible with their own various pagan practices. Indeed Constantine carried on marketing himself to the pagan majority of his subjects, minting coins featuring the 'Unconquered Sun god' and even allowing temples to be dedicated to his own divinity.

The support of the world's most powerful man made Christianity cool. More and more people flocked to follow the emperor's example. To be sure, the process took several decades. But by the late fourth century Christianity had become the dominant religion in the Roman world. We might like to think this had an enormous moral impact. The Romans did not, in fact, suddenly become paragons of virtue. They continued to torture people, although crucifixion was banned, and they carried on owning slaves on a massive scale. Constantine did make some improvements. Runaway slaves used to be branded on the face so they could be easily spotted if they tried to escape again. Now this practice was banned because the face had been created in the likeness of God and hence was sacrosanct. Instead they branded the feet. The Christian Constantine even invented new, enhanced punishments for those guilty of particularly heinous sexual crimes. Slaves who assisted in the kidnapping of virgins (I have no idea how big a social problem this was) were now to have molten lead poured down their throats.

Christianity itself was forced to change. A patron as powerful as the emperor was hard to say no to. He stuck his nose into all aspects of the church's affairs. Prior to his conversion, the Christian Church had been a loosely bound collection of local communities. There was no central authority. Constantine's conversion changed all that. Now the emperor wanted his new religion to be clear about what it believed. Christianity was a religion of the book and of the word, so surely it should be able to write down clearly what exactly it was that it believed? Matters came to a head when an Egyptian priest called Arius argued that the Trinity was not composed of three equals: the Father, the Son and the Holy Ghost. Surely, he argued, the Father must be superior to the Son. The father/son relationship was one of the core building blocks of ancient social relations. Sons obeyed their fathers. It seemed natural to many that God the Father was senior to his Son. In addition, God had created his son and sent him down from heaven; he must therefore have pre-existed him in some way. As for the Holy Ghost, well, he seemed to be no more than a glorified Mr Fixit. Arius's argument seemed perfectly reasonable to many.

The problem was that it smacked of a return to good old pagan polytheism. Wasn't Christianity meant to have only one God? Yet here, it appeared that three separate bits of divinity were doing their stuff independently. For Constantine, who by now was sole ruler of the whole empire, this division was unacceptable. He wanted his Christian empire to have one God whose sole representative on earth was the one emperor himself. Constantine duly summoned the bishops, about two hundred of whom poured into the city of Nicaea in northern Turkey in order to thrash the matter out. In the end it was the emperor himself who, supposedly, despite having no formal role in the church, came up with the solution. It was agreed that all three parts of the Trinity were 'consubstantial', all of the same matter. The Nicene Creed, which still defines Christian belief, was born. The three bishops who refused to go along with this were excommunicated and then exiled. Orthodoxy had been born too.

The impact of the emperor was to make the church much more materialistic. Money poured in through donations, legacies and tax breaks. There were great benefits from this financial bonanza. The church now had the resources to embark on a great building programme of churches, which were located in the prime urban sites, no longer the clandestine house churches of the times of persecution and repression. Whereas the church had previously been able to help only relatively small numbers of the poor, it now had the capacity to help tens of thousands. Lists were drawn up of the orphaned and the widowed, those who deserved to receive support. Bishops were given the authority to judge legal disputes if both parties agreed, acquiring a powerful and high-profile new leadership role as a result. Now that the church was respectable, men of talent and ambition wanted to join it and benefit from its attractive career prospects. The church was transformed from being an underground religion of the oppressed into a comfortable home for the wealthy classes.

Perhaps the main benefit for Christianity of Constantine's conversion was simple survival. If Christianity had remained a small sect I suspect it would eventually have died out like the many others that existed alongside it at the time: Manichaeism, Isis worship and Mithraism, to name only a few, all eventually died out without state backing. The downside for many ordinary Christians was a sense of overweening central intervention, a watering down of beliefs and purity of mission, and a moral conflict with the teachings of Jesus. Some marginal and provincial groups strongly resisted these centralising tendencies of the new Constantinian Church. In North Africa, for example, many in the local community refused to accept back into the church those who had betrayed it during Diocletian's persecutions. Constantine insisted they should. They saw this as a complete sell-out of their values. They broke away from the Orthodox Church and set up their own places of worship. Soon most towns and cities had two bishops – Orthodox and rebel. Within a few years of his conversion to Christianity, Constantine therefore found himself in the perverse situation of threatening and persecuting minority Christian groups because they refused to follow the official line.

Other Christians rejected society in a dramatic fashion

by becoming hermits. These religious extremists abandoned the settled life of the villages and towns to live in the deserts and uninhabited areas of the empire. One particularly tough holy man called Simeon stood for forty years on top of a pillar, which was about three feet wide. You won't be surprised to learn that this didn't do much for his feet, which became so worn out that the bones and sinews were visible. To make life even harder for himself, he carried out endless bowing and praying. One observer counted him doing 1,244 toe-touching supplications before God. In the end he gave up counting long before Simeon stopped his prostrations. Three of the joints of his spine were dislocated from this constant bending down. He ate so little that his poo looked like rabbit droppings and he even lost his eyesight for forty days from lack of nourishment. But for Simeon it was worth it. All of these trials showed that he was a true athlete of Christ. It moved him closer towards God.

One strange bonus of this proximity to God was that these holy men acquired a peculiar smell of their own. They completely rejected bathing as being too soft and luxurious. Baths were linked with their Roman conquerors, which made them doubly suspicious. Not washing for forty years generated a supersized level of BO: Simeon's stench was so strong that no one could get even halfway up the ladder towards him before being overpowered by it. Some of his disciples once forced themselves to go up to him but could only manage it after they covered their noses with incense and a strong-smelling ointment. Another holy man called Theodore spent two years alone in a cave. When he emerged, his head was covered in sores and pus, his hair was completely matted and an indescribable number of worms were lodged in it. He was so thin that his bones were all but visible through his flesh and he stank so badly that no one could stand near him.

But a smell that would probably make us vomit filled the ancients with wonder and awe. The terrible smell was seen as an 'odour of sanctity,' a sure sign that the holy man had achieved his goal of getting close to God. Now a man who is close to God is a powerful man. He acquires something of God's power, the means by which he can carry out His will on earth. In other words, the holy man became a miracle worker. From making it rain and driving off infestations of beetles to curing the lame and driving out demons, it was thought that these holy men could give the people the help they needed in difficult times. This was too great a power for the authorities and the Orthodox Church to leave untouched. Steadily they pulled back these extreme ascetics into settled communities, run by rules and controlled by the bishops. And in reality it was too harsh a lifestyle for all but the most fanatical to maintain. Most of these hermits were happy to follow a slightly softer option. In this way, the first monasteries were born.

Despite all these innovations, the late Roman empire is still widely characterised by Gibbon's narrative of decline and fall. Gibbon had his own agenda. He was concerned to learn the lessons of Rome's fall for the British empire in the aftermath of the American War of Independence. A complex historical process therefore became a vehicle for the discussion of all kinds of modern social ills. Someone with too much time on their hands has counted 210 different theories as to why the Roman empire ended, ranging from celibacy to cultural neurosis to lack of character.

But did it decline? There were many areas of innovation. New forms of art flourished, including intricate metalwork and the use of marble slabs to create strikingly modernist and impressionistic images. For the first time the law was codified into the great collections that formed the basis for many later European legal systems. The Christian Church continued to expand its mission, with new buildings and new forms of monasticism appearing, such as the Benedictine order.

And did it fall? Constantine had moved the capital to his new Christian city, Constantinople, in 330 AD. The empire had formally split into two in 395 AD. To be sure there was no emperor in the west after 476 AD but the eastern empire remained the biggest power in the Mediterranean and seems to have thrived economically until the bubonic plague and later Arab invasions. It is also worth noting that the eastern empire called itself 'Roman'. The term 'Byzantine' was not invented until the 1550s, a century after the fall of Constantinople in 1453. The decline and fall hypothesis may reflect western-centrism. The major European powers in the nineteenth century – Britain, France and Germany – assumed that their half of the empire must have been more important. Also, the eastern half had ended up under the control of Muslims and was therefore seen as lost beneath a layer of oriental despotism.

Even for those who lived in the western half of the empire, the whole image of barbarian invaders misrepresents the reality. Some writers like the Christian bishop

Salvian wrote about the higher moral qualities of the invading bands. It was the rapacious Roman governors he saw as the true barbarians. In any case, what did the end of the political unity of the western empire mean for most people? It was just a change of management for the agricultural poor who had always had a rough deal. Many of the wealthy landowners in places such as Gaul stayed in place, even if they had to hand over some of their property to the Goths. There were substantial areas of cultural continuity as well. The Christian Church remained a cornerstone of post-Roman western society. The barbarian settlers were, after all, Christian too. Slavery was another institution that remained. This is not to deny that the invading groups did cause substantial disruption and misery in some places. But if we simply see them as part of a downward spiral we will be getting a completely distorted picture.

The Roman empire was one of the most successful military and political institutions in history. We tend to focus on its heyday, when its armies were advancing and Rome's grip on power was tight. Yet the later period was the one where many of the institutions that dominated the medieval world were forged: law, monasteries and the Catholic Church. Like the Hellenistic period in the East, the later Roman empire has been overlooked and undervalued, seen as a period of military and political decline compared with the period of imperial expansion preceding it. In a postcolonial world, it is hard to sustain such biases in favour of periods of conquest.

The Hellenistic world and later Roman empire are but two examples. We could have looked at ancient Persia, the varied provincials of the Roman empire, or the Jews who spread out across the Mediterranean world in the diaspora. Or the 'barbarians' who bordered and interacted with Rome throughout the empire's life, and often contributed militarily to its survival. The Pharaohs of Egypt, the early Byzantine rulers and the successor kingdoms to the Roman state in the west could all have made an appearance in the discussion. The point is clear: the ancient world encompassed well over a thousand years of history across a huge land mass. To reduce that to a handful of acres around the Roman forum and the couple of decades either side of the building of the Parthenon is to overlook a thousand other possibilities for encountering the inhabitants of antiquity.

4

HOW DO WE DISCOVER IT?

Looking for a different kind of ancient world means using different approaches. Just as finding the common people involved examining a new range of texts, so new techniques can ask a whole different set of questions of the ancient evidence. Archaeology offers many new clues, as does science. It is not just modern technology that lets us see the ancient world afresh. We have already seen how the study of the senses can transform our understanding of how the ancients experienced their world. Psychiatry also has an important role to play in helping us to grasp the problems besetting ordinary people in the past. But before we start looking at these new forms of evidence, here's a basic question: how did the Romans generate energy?

WATERMILLS

One of the traditional views of the ancient world was that its energy supply was quite primitive. Above all, it was claimed that the ancients had no need to develop new sources of energy because they had a plentiful supply of cheap slaves. A few miles north of Arles in southern France lies an extraordinary piece of evidence that suggests the Romans did in fact harness a cheap and reliable energy source, which they put to productive use on an almost industrial scale. It is the watermill of Barbegal.

This is a large ruin that is hard to miss if you walk there. It was not, however, until 1940 that it was first properly examined: people had been too interested in artistic buildings and temples to bother with it. It probably dates from the fourth century AD, but there had been other structures before. The aqueduct that supplies the mill was built to supply fresh water from the nearby 'Little Alps' to the town of Arelate, as Arles was then known. At Barbegal the engineers faced a steep hill and the aqueduct divided. One arm went on to the town, the other cut through the top of the steep incline before flowing down the other side to power a total of sixteen waterwheels. The wheels were arranged in two rows of eight, one on each side of the water flow. Each row ran down the hillside so that the water cascaded from one wheel to the next before running off into a marsh a few hundred metres away.

The purpose of the mill was to grind flour. It could do this on a grand scale. One estimate, based on a water flow of 0.3 cubic metres per second, is that a wheel rotating ten times a minute at 65 per cent efficiency would drive a millstone fast enough to grind a

The Barbegal aqueduct

kilogram of flour per hour. This might not sound a lot but it all added up and the entire complex could produce four or five tonnes a day depending on how long it operated during daylight. Four or five tonnes of flour would have been enough to feed well over ten thousand people and means that the complex could probably have provided almost all the flour needs for the entire town of Arelate. The proximity of the wheels also meant that the milling complex could all be housed under one roof. It is hard not to see this as some kind of ancient factory.

Whether the mill was part of the original plan for the aqueduct is hard to say. One theory is that the aqueduct was first built to supply the town with water but it either eventually furred up or the quality of the water from the source deteriorated to such an extent as to be undrinkable. A new aqueduct was then built to resupply the town, and the old one was converted to supply the flour mill with an energy source where the quality of the water did not matter. It's not known who designed this great feat of engineering. There is a grave in Arles of a man called Quintus Candidius Benignus, who is described as being 'more clever than anyone, and none surpassed him in the construction of machines and the building of water channels'. It could be a coincidence but it almost seems too much of one for this not to be the engineer in question.

The milling complex consisted of the grinding wheels themselves in conjunction with a supply road for the delivery of unmilled grain and the removal of milled flour. The entire complex measures about 40 metres by 20 metres, about the size of a good-size modern industrial unit. The waterwheels were mounted on the outside of the walls of the complex. As ever with archaeology, a fair amount of creativity is required in order to resolve some of the remaining issues. For example, the slope of the ground on the hillside is 30 degrees but it would have needed to be greater in order to squeeze in eight wheels. One theory is that the section of the building at the top of the hill was raised up and the lowest sunk down and in this way the gradient of the hydraulic flow was increased. Another unknown quantity is whether the Romans used any gearing mechanism to increase the speed and efficiency of the milling process. All of this shows that the estimates on flour production are really just informed guesswork.

It is unclear exactly what kind of waterwheel was used. Wheels can be mounted horizontally or vertically. The Barbegal complex used vertical wheels, as they were wall-mounted, but it is impossible to detect whether they were undershot or overshot. Undershot wheels sit directly in the water flow whereas overshot wheels have the water flow delivered by a chute to the top of the wheel, which is then driven by a combination of the flow of the water and gravity. Overshot is much the more efficient system, but this may not have been an issue if there was a plentiful supply of water. The aqueduct flow was steady but modest and if the theory that it had silted up is correct then there would probably have been a need for an efficient overshot system.

Technical issues aside, Barbegal challenges the view that the ancients made little use of the technology they did possess because of the availability of slave power. They may have been great philosophers but the ancients were certainly slow to turn their intellects towards practical problems of power supply. They didn't invent windmills, for example, and don't seem to have managed to combine the wheel and the pivot to make a wheelbarrow. Nor is it clear that they made extensive use of watermills, only a few of which have been discovered. This could just be an accident of history. The Domesday book records 5,624 watermills in England but evidence of only about a dozen still survives. The dearth of surviving Roman watermills might be accounted for by our indifference or inattention to such structures, as was the case with Barbegal. One traditional explanation for their apparent absence was that the Mediterranean area lacked the steady flowing streams needed to turn them. As at Barbegal, though, an aqueduct can do the job nicely and there was no shortage of them in the Roman world. Mills didn't even need a dedicated water supply, as the water could simply flow on to the town after it had driven the wheels. This is what seems to have happened in another mill complex on the side of the Janiculum hill in Rome.

But for all that, it is still true that the ancients made less use of their available technology than they could have. Did the presence of slaves make them lazy, giving them time to sit about philosophising? Well, for one thing, slaves, while cheap during Rome's great conquests, were in peacetime expensive both to buy and maintain. A more mundane explanation is that it probably cost too much to transport grain in quantities by land to mills. It was only in unique situations, where there happened to be an easy water source in a fertile area close by a large urban market, that it made sense to develop economies of scale. Barbegal is not quite unique but there are only a handful of examples of similar structures. It may be that many more are just waiting to be discovered. Or perhaps their absence indicates the limits of the ancient mentality when it came to power generation.

BONES

New scientific techniques allow us to re-examine existing evidence to see what more it can reveal. One example of this is the bones of the victims at Pompeii and Herculaneum, the towns that sat close by Vesuvius when it erupted in 79 AD. I refer not to those dramatic plaster casts created from the empty spaces left in the ash deposit by the decayed bodies of the dead, but to the approximately fifteen hundred skeletons that have been uncovered in the two towns. They supply us with quantitative, cross-social data that is unavailable from any other source.

'Skeletons' is actually not the right word. Although some of the Pompeian victims' remains have been kept in the condition in which they were discovered, most were reburied, stored badly or taken away to be housed in private collections. The majority were eventually piled up in an ancient bath building, the Terme del Sarno, which is located south of the forum in Pompeii. The human bones had been dumped with various animal bones, such as those of horses and dogs. Over time, the skeletons have become disarticulated, meaning they simply fell apart to become a collection of individual bones. This makes it almost impossible to tell which bones go together.

The reason for this neglect is that when Pompeii was rediscovered in the eighteenth century people were most fascinated by the wall paintings, mosaics and other collectable artefacts. The public were interested in the human remains but not in skeletons as such. What people loved were the stories that could be attached to the bones. Often the victims were found holding on to precious items they were taking with them while trying to flee. It all brought home the human side of the disaster. Skeletons were sometimes used simply to impress visiting VIPs. In 1768 the Austrian emperor visited Pompeii. A house was named in his honour and he came to witness the excavations taking place. The workmen removed the stones to reveal a kitchen where a skeleton lay artfully sprawled across the amphorae. It was preposterous. The emperor saw it for the sham it was and was not amused.

Even though skeletons stopped being used as marketing props, a tendency soon arose to create elaborate tales about who these individuals had been and how they had met their death. In one of the best examples, a skeleton found in 1763 close to the Herculaneum Gate was claimed to have been in a sentry box, holding a lance and surrounded by armour. The widely accepted interpretation was that this was a Roman soldier of such discipline that, even in the midst of the eruption, he would not desert his post without permission. It was a story the British loved, as it symbolised the kind of devotion an empire needed if it were to be great. The problem is that there is no evidence that a skeleton was even found in this location. Then the sentry box turned out to be a funerary monument. So if he did exist – which is possible, as many items went missing in the early excavations – this was most likely to have been some random Pompeian taking shelter in a tomb.

One of the big differences between Pompeii and Herculaneum was that prior to 1982 very few bones had been

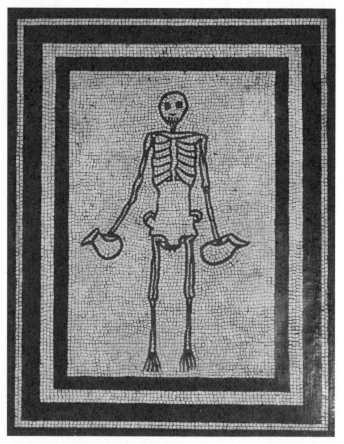

A mosaic of a skeleton from Pompeii

discovered at Herculaneum. It was assumed that almost everyone had managed to escape by sea before the town was covered by volcanic mud. The speed of the alleged evacuation was suggested by the fact that the few bodies that had been discovered were of vulnerable persons, such as a baby who had been abandoned in a wooden cradle. But then bodies were discovered on the beachfront – about 380 bodies, lying in heaps, killed as they tried to flee by sea.

Many of the bodies from both towns display what is called the 'pugilistic' position: that is they have their arms stuck out like a boxer. This is characteristic of a body that has been exposed to very high heat at death. What the bodies from the two towns are saying is that it was the super-hot pyroclastic surges from the volcano that were the real killers, not the ash. Rather than being slowly suffocated, most victims were killed instantly by exposure to surges that reached 250 degrees Celsius in Pompeii and 400 degrees in Herculaneum. There was nowhere for them to hide. The fact that bodies have additionally been discovered under roofing material and walls suggests that some will have been killed by the buildings they were sheltering in collapsing under the weight of the falling ash.

The bones challenge modern assumptions that it would be young, healthy males who were most likely to survive the disaster. In Herculaneum, the bodies found by the beach show a strong bias in favour of women and young children. But in Pompeii there seems to be a roughly even number of men and women among the victims. What is most noticeable in the more recent Herculaneum finds is that the men died on the beach, presumably in a desperate attempt to launch boats out onto the sea, while the women and children sat huddled together under the brick arches that ran along the shoreline.

The lack of any obvious bias in the adult victims in Pompeii by way of age or sex may be because the final volcanic surges happened with such speed that there would have been no chance for anyone to escape no matter how fit or strong. But what we don't know is what percentage of the population died in the disaster. About 1,100 bodies have been found in Pompeii, while estimates for the size of the population range from six thousand to thirty thousand. Either way, a considerable majority of Pompeians have not been found. They might all have left the town in the days, months and even years before. The eruption had been brewing for some time, with tremors being felt, so perhaps most people had already left. And there had been a major earthquake in 62 AD, which may have meant many had already abandoned the town. Or perhaps their bodies are still lying in the ash, waiting to be discovered as they were in Herculaneum.

The bones can tell us something about the level of health in the population. Teeth are particularly useful in this respect. Dental hygiene was almost non-existent in the ancient world but then sugar was much less widely used. A sample of the victims' jaws in Pompeii showed that well over half had lost a tooth when they were alive. One upper jaw had lost no fewer than fourteen teeth. This tooth loss might have been the result of decay or simply old age. The incidence of caries was actually lower than we might have anticipated, with about 15 per cent of the teeth showing signs of decay. The Herculaneum skeletons showed that only one person in two had a decaying tooth. However, as people have their teeth pulled out if the decay is severe, and are therefore missing from the skeletons, it's hard to say how good this picture is.

Another piece of dental evidence comes from the formation of the enamel during childhood. Irregularities can occur as a result of poor nutrition, infection or other trauma. This linear enamel hypoplasia, as it is termed, can therefore act as an indicator of the healthiness of a child's upbringing. Perhaps 50 per cent of teeth exhibited this defect, but results have varied significantly from sample to sample. Probably all we can say is that periods of significant illness and poor nutrition seem to have been reasonably commonplace in the average Pompeian childhood. This may have resulted in the growth of many of these individuals being stunted. But in many cases only a slight level of damage to the enamel can be detected and so any impact on the individual's stature may well have been equally limited. As yet, the evidence from the teeth is inconclusive. We should be particularly careful, then, not to extrapolate too much from this regarding the general level of childhood health in the ancient world.

The bones provide little evidence for the population's average age. There is some evidence in the Pompeian sample of various age-related disorders, such as bony growths on the skull, which tend to occur in post-menopausal women, but this condition is virtually absent in Herculaneum. Some individuals will have lived into old age no matter how low the level of overall life expectancy. Comparative evidence from other pre-industrial societies suggests that people in the ancient world had short life spans, with only 6.7 per cent living to be over 60, 2 per cent over 70, and just 0.25 per cent over 80. The bones in Pompeii and Herculaneum do nothing to suggest whether or not these figures are too pessimistic.

Other surviving bones from the ancient world can tell us about the perilous lives of their owners. One gladiator graveyard in York contains 80 skeletons of men who probably died fighting in the arena. The skeletons were taller than the average Briton and were heavily built. A third of the specimens had one arm which was two inches or more longer than the other. This was the result of the endless practice with a heavy sword. Many of the skeletons have blunt-force wounds. One victim even has the tooth marks of a large carnivore, such as a bear or a lion, on its pelvis. Forty-five of the skeletons appear to have been beheaded. This may be the result of execution or it could reflect a local form of delivering the coup de grâce to a defeated gladiator.

Another gladiator cemetery in Ephesus shows similar traits. Many of the sixty-eight skeletons have head wounds. Eleven had head injuries that had healed over, meaning they had been suffered in a previous bout. Ten had suffered head wounds that were probably the cause of death. Gladiators all wore protective helmets, apart from the net-fighter, but the force of the blow was sufficient to pierce the armour. Three skulls had been pierced by a trident, which is the weapon a net-fighter carried. If a gladiator lost and his plea for mercy was given the thumbs down – although we can't be certain about the direction, it may have been thumbs up – then he was expected to die properly. Lying on the ground, he had to throw his head back and expose his neck. His victorious opponent would then thrust the sword down through the throat and into the heart. Some of the vertebrae of the skeletons at Ephesus have cut marks that probably resulted from this downward stabbing motion.

The bones can tell us something about what these poor men ate. They trained hard and ate a diet that was high in carbohydrate – gladiator food was sometimes called 'stuffing' – because it helped them to put on a lot of weight. Partly the weight gain was from muscle but it was from fat, too. As with Japanese Sumo wrestlers, fat was thought to be an advantage. The point of the endless carb-loading was not only for weight gain but to provide the gladiator with a protective layer of blubber. Like Sumo wrestlers, gladiators were fit and muscular. This well-honed physique was covered with subcutaneous fat that softened any blows the fighter might receive. Cuts in fatty flesh produce a lot of blood but do little damage to the more important nerves and veins below. They don't hurt as much either, which meant that the gladiator was able to carry on fighting if he suffered a minor wound. It may also have resulted in lots of blood and gore, which is partly what the spectators came to see.

The problem with a carbohydrate-rich diet was that it left the gladiators deficient in calcium. This was a problem because calcium helps keep bones strong, and gladiators needed strong bones to support their heavy physiques. As a consequence, they took food supplements in the form of bone and wood ash, which are rich in calcium. Not that appealing, I know, but analysis of the bones in Ephesus shows that it had the desired effect and raised the gladiators' calcium levels to well above those of the general population.

DOWN THE DRAINS

Looking at skeletons can tell us a lot about a population's overall nutrition, what kind of physical stresses they faced, and what kinds of disease they suffered from. How can we use science to find out about what kinds of things ordinary people ate? We have plenty of literary references to food, but these tend to focus on the high-quality delicacies that were served, or reputedly served, at banquets. We have very little evidence about what the average person ate. Luckily, in Herculaneum a sewer has survived. The walls of this drain are encrusted with the desiccated faecal remains of the town's inhabitants.

One of the difficulties with conserving the site of Herculaneum is that it sits deep below the modern ground level, meaning that rainwater has to be constantly drained away. It was decided to clear out an original Roman sewer to help with this task – which shows how good Roman engineering was – the idea being to run some new plastic pipes along its length. Before the pipes were laid, environmental archaeologists examined the contents of the sewer to see if they could shed any light on what the Roman diet consisted of.

The sewer wasn't just covered with faecal remains. All kinds of scraps, leftovers and bits had been thrown down the town's latrine holes. Over time these had built up in what was, in effect, a cesspit. Normally, these sewers would have been emptied, probably by slaves, with the muck being dumped outside the town or used to fertilise the fields. The volcanic eruption meant that the pits were left covered just as they were, contents and all. Half-chewed fish bones, bits of goose eggshell, and fragments of bone were all found. Of course the fact that these remains are of animal products may indicate that we are dealing with the better-off citizens of Herculaneum, which was in any case a pretty well-heeled place, acting as a holiday resort on the bay of Naples for the well-off to escape from the noise and smell of Rome. The sewer was actually located beneath a relatively modest block of shops and flats, which makes it unlikely that we are talking about the diet of the super-rich. So what conclusions can be drawn from this remarkable if unpleasant evidence?

The first is that most of what the Romans ate was locally sourced and supplied. Some of the mollusc shells found in the sewers came directly from the town's beach. Transport was expensive and many foods would deteriorate quickly, particularly in the summer, so the cheapest and easiest course was to eat what was on your doorstep. Lots of fish bones and bits of sea urchin were found too. If you lived on the margins of the great fish basket that was the Mediterranean Sea, then this was the obvious place to turn for your daily bread, as it were. There were lots of figs in the drains as well, which was probably because they were in season at the time of the eruption, although the exact date is unclear.

But not everything was locally produced. Grain was probably imported from Egypt, which supplied Rome as well. Other more luxurious items included dates from North

Africa. Pepper was also found, which had been imported from India. Roman traders sailed to India on the monsoon winds, which could be dangerous but was all the more profitable for being so. Before you assume that this made it wildly expensive and exotic, bear in mind that pepper was a popular spice in Rome and was imported in bulk. The Roman writer Pliny the Elder, who died during the eruption of Vesuvius when he sailed closer to have a better view, complained that he couldn't understand why pepper was so popular when 'it only has bitterness to recommend it'. Black pepper of the sort found in the sewer was the cheapest type. It was used to spice up drinks and is even found in the Roman fort at Vindolanda near Hadrian's Wall. In Rome it was stored in a specially constructed warehouse, which still partly survives under the Basilica of Constantine. The quantities were so large that when Alaric the Goth held Rome to ransom in 408 AD part of the deal to buy him off was 3,000 lbs of pepper. This sounds a lot but it probably didn't cost a fortune because it was such a common import.

It's not clear how much meat there was. Lots of bits of eggshell were found but this doesn't mean that they ate the chickens that laid them. Pork seems to have been the meat of choice: the rubbish dumps from around Pompeii were full of pig bones. Its popularity can be gauged from the fact that in the later empire the citizens of Rome were given a free pork handout of 5 lbs for five months of the year. It wasn't enough to live off but it was, in the words of one imperial law, a handy 'titbit' which could cheer up the inhabitants. Pigs often feature in Roman humour, presumably because of their importance to Roman cuisine. One widely known text was a parody of a will written by a piglet. The unlucky animal, about to be eaten at a feast, leaves his innards to the sausage-makers, his bladder to the boys (to inflate and use as a ball), and his bristles to the cobblers (presumably to use as a brush). He asks that his dead body be cared for well, including being nicely seasoned with pepper.

So far it all sounds like a healthy Mediterranean diet (except for the lack of tomatoes, pasta and oranges). But there were some unpleasant things lurking in the remains from the sewers as well. Grain weevils seem to have survived the milling process and were eaten by unsuspecting bread-eaters. The presence of fly pupae highlights that ancient notions of food hygiene were basic at best, and certainly different from our own. Eating fresh food was probably the best way to avoid food poisoning.

Lead poisoning seems to have been a problem. Lead is a dangerous poison that accumulates in the body. Repeated exposure to even small amounts can have a serious negative impact on health and can even increase violent and delinquent behaviour. We all know that the Romans used lead to make their water pipes. It was even once argued that lead poisoning caused the Roman empire to fall. This cataclysmic view was later revised when it became clear that water pipes developed a layer of calcium carbonate called sinter, which protected the drinking water from lead contamination. However, a recent study of ninety-two skeletons from Herculaneum has shown that these bodies did indeed have exceptionally high levels of lead contamination. Their average concentration of 83 parts per million is higher than that found even in long-term workers in lead factories.

How is this to be explained? The lead wasn't coming from the water source or from its distribution points. Using a sophisticated and snappily titled technique called 'Laser ablation inductively coupled plasma mass spectronomy', it has been possible to analyse how the sinter deposits took a while to build up, and that during this period dangerously high levels of lead were entering the water supply. This was important because a complex system of water supply was always having repairs and replacements. This was particularly true after the earthquake that hit Pompeii in 62 AD, which will have necessitated large-scale repair work. In short, the Pompeians may have been eating well but their water was poisoning them.

MENTAL HEALTH

So far we've focused on the physical effects of ancient life on the body. Now I want to think about the impact on the mind. What mental pressures did people face and how can we go about assessing the level of mental health in the ancient world?

Living in the ancient world could be exceptionally stressful. Death was a regular visitor to most communities and we have seen that mortality rates were likely to have been higher than those in any less developed country in the world today. This was not because of a shortage of food, although this could clearly sometimes happen. It was because of a lack of hygiene, poor sanitation, widespread disease and the absence of any effective medicines to combat it. This combination of factors intensified the physical pressure on people, leaving them less able to cope with the mental pressures they faced. Where you find bad physical health you find in parallel a much higher incidence of bad mental health.

Life was hard in both the city and the country. Urban life forced people to live in overcrowded conditions and left them vulnerable to crime. Economic migrants can be expected to have suffered more than most because they had left behind their family and wider kinship support networks. People had plenty of financial worries. Debt problems seem to have been widespread because borrowing from the ancient equivalent of the loan shark was the only way to tide yourself over during a financial crisis. Many, perhaps a majority, lived just above the breadline and had very few reserves to fall back on if times got tough. There was no social security net. If the family fell on hard times all it could do was sell everything, including the kids, and beg for a living.

Military service could, as always, be traumatic. For example, it has been estimated that in the second century BC over half of all Roman men served in the army for an average of seven years. Under the first emperor, Augustus, about one-sixth of all male Italian citizens performed military service for twenty years. Rome was a military machine. But it wasn't just Rome. All ancient societies expected their menfolk to fight in order to further their communal interests, and warfare was a normal part of the social landscape. Wars could of course be particularly traumatic for civilians on the receiving end. Rebellions were crushed with heartless brutality. Defeated cities could expect to see their men of fighting age executed and their women and children sold off into slavery.

Disasters were fairly regular events. We tend to think of the high points of ancient success, whether it is the Battle of Marathon or Julius Caesar's conquest of Gaul. But the ancient world also suffered regular crises, ranging from military defeats, like the Roman defeat at Cannae when fifty thousand men fell in a single day, to earthquakes, great fires like the one that hit Rome in 64 AD (when, contrary to the myth, Nero did not fiddle), food shortages, floods and plagues such as the one that devastated Athens in the Peloponnesian War. Small-scale accidents were common on building sites, where Health and Safety was not the norm, as was the risk of violent assault and robbery in daily life.

Ancient society could be really nasty. People tried to make sure they had enough to survive and they don't seem to have had much time to pity anyone worse off than themselves. If a woman was raped, she bore the shame of having been violated. In a Roman story about a young girl who dies after having an abortion, it is clear that there was no sympathy for her. As her body was carried to the funeral people shouted 'she got what she deserved!' And we have seen how brutal the treatment could be of slaves. Being a slave was like being a donkey: life consisted of beatings, hard work and not much food. Then there was the sexual abuse. Even ex-slaves were notorious for treating their slaves cruelly, presumably a way of compensating for the mistreatment they themselves had received.

Can we assess the impact of all this societal stress on the

ancient mind? It's very difficult to measure the incidence of mental disorders even in the modern world. In America, for example, there is a 48 per cent lifetime prevalence rate for psychiatric disorders, meaning that almost half of all people suffer from a mental disorder at some point in their lives. The most common are major depression (17.1 per cent), alcoholism (14.1 per cent), social phobia (13.3 per cent), and simple phobia (11.3 per cent). If you look at other cultures, however, you find conflicting data (major depression hits only 2.9 per cent of South Koreans in their life). This is because cultures respond to mental health problems differently and strong societal pressures can exist to repress the symptoms. Psychiatry itself is a relatively new discipline and there is a great deal of disagreement about what constitutes mental disorder, what causes it, and how it should be treated. Some so-called disorders seem quite minor. I think I suffer from 'disorder of written expression' (bad handwriting) and both my children could sometimes be said to display 'oppositional defiant disorder', described as defiant acts by children such as temper tantrums, being annoying or angry.

All of this makes it impossible to supply data about mental health in the ancient world. But modern research does show that there is a strong correlation between the level of social stress an individual suffers and the state of their mental health. Put simply, if you are put under a lot of pressure you are more likely to show the strain and maybe even crack. The high level of everyday stress that people in the ancient world encountered throughout their lives means that we can reasonably expect their mental health to have been poor. That theirs seems to have been a world in which people were taught, by and large, to suppress their emotions will not have helped.

Research also shows a clear correlation between socio-economic status and mental health: the lower down the scale you sit, the more stress you are likely to suffer, the worse your mental health is likely to be, and the fewer resources you'll have to cope with it. We can conclude that the worst off in the ancient world – slaves, the destitute, widows, many of the old – had levels of mental health well below the norm.

Perhaps we could argue that people in the ancient world were generally tougher than their modern counterparts and therefore coped better with these stresses. Evidence certainly exists to support the claim that some people are capable of great resilience and that some cultures promote psychological robustness (think stiff upper lip and legendary Spartan toughness). In fact the ancients leave plenty of evidence that they did suffer from mental disorders. Ancient medical writers have numerous accounts of patients suffering from various kinds of delusional disorders. Galen describes a patient who thought he was a pot and was scared he would break. Another believed he was a chicken, and another identified himself with Atlas, bearing the burden of the world on his shoulders. One patient bound up her little finger because she was worried that the world would collapse if she bent it. One writer treats homosexuality as a mental disorder, but the same was true of the American Psychiatric Association in the 1950s. Some treatments could be severe. Celsus advises that the insane are best treated by certain tortures. Others were sympathetic and gentle.

Aretaeus writes about a wealthy man who lived in constant fear of losing his money and status. The doctor arranged for pretend legacies to be announced to him from time to time as a way of relieving his anxiety. Phrenologists studied the shape and features of the head to reveal its inner heat: too much heat and moisture in the brain would lead to madness and would be reflected in thick, black hair. Bald people, by contrast, had cool, dry brains, which made their hair wither but helped to keep them sane.

But these kinds of medical theories were largely reserved for the wealthy in Roman society. Doctors were expensive. Most people explained mental illness in terms of demonic possession. That is not to say that demons were regarded merely as the cause of mental disorder – they were also seen as divine agents who could fulfil a variety of religious purposes. Nor was anyone really sure what a demon was: unclean spirits of the underworld or the souls of those who had met a violent death were two common explanations. It was certainly easy to become infected. One man was simply standing outside his inn when a black dog came up, stood in front of him and yawned, which made the man yawn in turn, whereupon the dog immediately disappeared through his mouth and he was gripped by spasms. This belief, incidentally, may be the origin of our custom of putting a hand in front of the mouth when yawning.

The treatment for this kind of demonic invasion of the body was to try to drive the demons back out. Some approaches relied on strong-arm physical tactics, including beatings, trepanations (drilling holes in the head), and venesections (bloodletting). Others looked to magical incantations, spells and exorcisms. One spell, described as an 'excellent rite for driving out demons', calls on the evil spirit to leave: 'I conjure you, demon, whoever you are, by this god, SABARBARBATHIOTH SABARBARBATHIO-UTH SABARBARBATHIONETH SABARBARBAPHAI. Come out, demon, whoever you are, and stay away from him.' The magic words, like abracadabra, were meant to speak directly to the demonic powers in their own language.

Some disorders, which we would regard as having a mental cause, were explained by the ancients in physical terms. Hysteria, for example, was thought to be an affliction of women caused by the womb's propensity to wander in the body. Found mainly in virgins and widows, the symptoms included panic attacks and seizures. Its treatment consisted of the application of strong smells to try either to lure the uterus back down or drive it up again into its proper place. Magic could also be used: 'I conjure you, O womb … do not gnaw into the heart like a dog, but remain in your own intended and proper place.' It is hard not to see the wandering womb as a metaphor for the dangers of female social mobility in Roman society. Women faced irresistible pressure to reproduce and rear children. The physical and emotional stress this generated will have overwhelmed many. Hysteria offered a way for these women to express their inner distress.

The ancients had various explanations as to what caused mental disorder. But they lacked the very language of psychiatric expression that we have today. They understood it in a variety of physical and religious ways, all of which were completely different from our own. Modern research into mental health tells us to expect a high incidence of mental disorders as a result of the high level of stress and hierarchy in the ancient world. What it can't do is to predict the form in which those disorders would have been expressed, treated or viewed.

5

DID GREECE AND ROME MATTER?

Think of the ancient world and it is the glory that was Greece and the grandeur that was Rome that seem to stand out as shining beacons of civilisation in a sea of barbarism. They appear isolated, cut off from the world around them. When we do notice cultural contact it tends to be that which took place between the Greeks and the Romans or with their conquered subjects. The ancient world needs to be seen in a broader context. It has to be fitted in with the global history of its day. What did the Persians think of the Greeks, for example, or what kind of cultural contact existed between the two? And comparisons can be made with other empires of the time. How does the Roman empire stack up in comparison with ancient China; and was it more or less centralised, run efficiently or justly, in comparison with that empire in the east? Comparing them with other pre-industrial societies lets us see what was truly unique about Greece and Rome.

DID THE GREEKS AND PERSIANS HATE EACH OTHER?

The story of the Persian invasions of Greece is an epic tale. Twice the Persian king – Darius in 490 and his son Xerxes in 480 – had tried to make the collection of independent Greek states yield to the might of the Persian empire. Twice the king had been repulsed by the freedom-loving Greeks, who had put aside their differences in order to resist the overwhelming forces of a barbarian autocrat. In fact the victory was such an achievement that it needed something even greater than an epic poem to record it. The result was that history itself was born when Herodotus, the 'Father of History', sat down to write an account of what it was about the Greeks that had enabled them to pull off such a magnificent feat.

All the ancient sources we have for the wars are from the Greek side. There is no Persian point of view. Of course, that's mainly because the Greeks won. History is written by the winners. In the same way that you rarely hear references to the World Wars in Germany, the Persians had a vested

interest in forgetting the wars against the Greeks, which means that we're trying to understand the past from a highly biased set of records. It would be like trying to write a history of the Troubles in Northern Ireland using only nationalist or unionist sources. The very fact that the wars are traditionally called the *Persian* Wars underlines how we

Relief of the Persian king Xerxes in the doorway of his palace at Persepolis in the West have been strongly biased in favour of seeing the affair through Greek eyes.

Now there are good political and ideological reasons for this. Democracy, albeit in a far more radical form, was invented in some Greek city-states, where freedom was valued highly, and the flowering of intellectual creativity in this period underpins much of the western tradition. But if we want to understand what the Greek victory meant in the context of the ancient world, then we need to look at the bigger picture.

For a start, we should not overstate the importance of the wars for the Persians. The Achaemenid empire, as it is also known, had been established by Cyrus the Great in the sixth century BC. At the time of the wars, it had an estimated population of 50 million. The *Guinness Book of Records* is confident enough in these numbers to claim that this represented 44 per cent of the world's population at the time, making it the most successful empire in global history. Hopefully, the previous chapters will have underlined just how questionable these figures are. However spurious the accolade might be, it is safe to say that the Persian empire was enormous, stretching from Egypt to Bulgaria and from the Black Sea to the river Indus. The wars against the Greeks succeeded in putting a stop to Persian attempts to expand into Europe, but they represented only a minor front for what was a truly global empire. The absence of Persian histories of the war may not just have reflected the fact of Persian defeat. They may have reflected Persian indifference.

Think of the wars and it is the two great battles of Marathon and Thermopylae that spring to mind. In the first, in

490 BC, the Athenians and Plataeans defeated the numerically far greater Persian army under the command of Datis and Artaphernes. Note that the Persian king did not bother himself to attend. This was perhaps the first indication that the war was not quite the epic contest the Greek histories might lead us to believe. Neither were the battles simply the result of a sudden unexpected invasion by the Persian forces. The Persian and Greek worlds had been colliding for over half a century since Cyrus had conquered the Greek cities on the coast of Ionia, in what is now Turkey. These fiercely independent city-states proved difficult to rule and in the end the Persians set up individual tyrants over each of the towns to keep them quiet.

One of these local rulers, a Greek called Aristagoras, wanted to expand his power by invading the nearby Greek island of Naxos. The Persians provided military and financial backing for the enterprise but it was a disaster. Realising that the Persians would fire him as a result, Aristagoras did what any honourable politician would do. He changed sides. Calling on all the other Greek cities that were living under the Persian yoke, he incited them to throw it off. The Ionian revolt was born. Other more distant Greeks were drawn into the struggle. The powerful city of Athens entered, looking to increase its influence in the region and to keep the Persians well away from the mainland. In 498 BC the combined Greek forces ransacked the Persian capital in the region, Sardis. It was a terrible insult to the great Persian king, Darius, who vowed to have vengeance.

Sure enough, Darius got his way. When the Ionians were crushed in battle in 494 BC, the rebellion was stamped out.

Now Darius wanted to go further and punish the mainland Greeks for their insolence in interfering with so great an empire and burning one of its fine cities. The Persian invasion began two years before Marathon, with the occupation of the northern Greek territories of Thrace and Macedon. A second force was sent in 490 but after some initial successes, this was routed by the Athenians at Marathon. Darius now decided that it was time to eradicate this troublesome region on his European flank. But it was left to his son Xerxes to persevere with the plan after his father's death in 486. Xerxes took his responsibility seriously and in 480 took personal command of an enormous army, probably one of the largest ever seen in the ancient world, which does not, of course, mean that it was any good. Victorious at Thermopylae over the Greek alliance, the Persians sacked Athens and took control of much of the mainland. But the Greeks were above all a naval power. They destroyed the Persian fleet at the Battle of Salamis, which allowed them to take the upper hand on land too. After defeating them at Plataea, the Greeks drove the Persians out and the invasion was over.

The war, however, was not. The allied Greek forces took advantage of the Persian weakness to drive them out of Greece altogether. Under Athenian leadership, the alliance known as the Delian League continued to campaign against Persia for another thirty years. Gone were the Persians from Europe; and, after the Battle of Eurymedon in 466, from Ionia. But not gone from Egypt, where the League's support for a revolt came to nothing, nor from Cyprus, where a League fleet sailed in 451. It was only then that the half-century of Greco-Persian conflicts finally came to an end.

Certainly, it was an embarrassment for the Persians to have failed to subdue a few small cities. It was not the main problem they faced by the mid-fifth century, however. Internal conflict was weakening the Persian state from within, so they adopted a new political policy of trying to cause divisions among the Greeks: if the Greeks were split then they could not pose a threat to the Persians. They bribed Greeks to vote in particular ways in their city assemblies and continually interfered in order to foster animosity between the two main Greek powers, Sparta and Athens. This was not a difficult thing to do. The Greek city-states were always at each other's throats and Sparta had become deeply suspicious of Athens's rise to power at the head of the Delian League. The Persian policy came to fruition when the Greeks tore themselves apart in the long Peloponnesian War of 431–404 BC, which left Athenian power in tatters. All this time Persia was left well alone. As one later Greek historian, Plutarch, put it, the Greeks were too busy fighting among themselves to fight against the 'barbarians'.

Were they really barbarians? The Persian empire was certainly autocratic but unsophisticated it was not. It had a centralised system of administration, which used a single language, to control and help unify its disparate ethnic groups. Its large civil service enabled the central monarch to exercise his rule across his lands. Like the later Romans, the Persians built a large network of roads to facilitate communications with the centre, to allow for more rapid troop movements, and to help form the empire into a more cohesive single entity. You could argue that it needed an autocratic form of government to rule such a diverse empire. As the Greeks discovered after Alexander's conquest, democracy was alright for a small city-state where everyone shared the same background but it was no use if you were trying to manage an empire. We should be careful then not to accept the traditional Greek view of the Persians as a bunch of barbarians. This attitude – the kind of hostile approach to anything foreign that is still found today wherever there is conflict – was commonplace during and immediately after the wars. But it is not an accurate representation of the relationship between the two cultures.

There may have been wars, but there was extensive cultural and trade contact too, and as much dialogue as conflict. The Persian kings were not trying to ethnically cleanse the world of Greek culture. In the Greek-influenced areas of their kingdom, they supported the construction of Greek temples and Greek-style buildings. They respected some Greek works of art so much that they were housed in the royal archives. And the Greeks reciprocated this interest in the other's culture. They imported its luxury goods, sought employment in its empire, and artisans copied Persian styles. Intellectual ideas were swapped as well. The Greek philosopher Anaxagoras even went to Athens to lecture about Persian astronomical theories.

The Greeks were too sophisticated to see the Persians as simple barbarians. They knew that they were dealing with a successful global empire. The writer Xenophon, for example, portrayed them as reasonable, moderate, and, in the case of Cyrus, model rulers. He praises the Persian king for his administrative skills. We have seen how, later, Alexander the Great showed respect for both Persian culture and their kings, even if this was driven by the political need for accommodation. Interaction between the two worlds was complex and rich in meaning. The Athenians and Persians did not hate each other. If we focus on the wars and belittle the Persians as a barbaric enemy, then we are missing all of this, and seeing only the Greek jingoistic view, which prevailed in the period after the wars and would always get a hearing in some quarters. In reality, the Greco-Persian wars were themselves a product of cultural contacts between the two peoples. To that extent the Greeks mattered because of their proximity to the Persians.

CHINA AND ROME

At the time of the first emperor, Augustus, Rome dominated the Mediterranean world. At the same time, the Han empire controlled the central plains of Northern China. Both were huge. They covered broadly the same area – about twenty times the size of Britain or half that of America. Their populations, at 60 million, were about the same size. Between them, these two great empires ruled as much as half of the world's population.

But they knew almost nothing about each other. The great distance between the two meant that such contact as took place was usually indirect. Luxury goods like silk and Roman glassware were traded by middlemen through the Persian empire, which sat between them. As the two empires conquered more lands, with the Romans taking the ancient Near East at about the same time as China moved west into central Asia, the geographical gap between them narrowed. However it always remained too far and too blocked by other powers for either side to get any clear picture of what the other was like.

But they did know of each other's existence, and contact was attempted. In 97 BC the Chinese general Ban Chao tried to send an envoy to Rome but it failed; and according to ancient Chinese historians, the Romans sent several embassies to China. The first arrived in 166 AD, sent by the emperor 'An-tun', presumably Antoninus, which could refer either to Antoninus Pius or Marcus Aurelius, who was also an Antonine. The embassy came bearing gifts of elephant tusks, rhinoceros horn and tortoise shell, but the Chinese were so unimpressed by these commonplace offerings that they started to suspect that Rome was not quite as rich as they had been led to believe. Another source records that in 226 AD a Roman merchant made it to a place near modern Hanoi. The local prefect sent him to the emperor Sun Quan who asked him what his homeland and its people were like. The emperor even organised an expedition that attempted to send the merchant back to Rome with a Chinese

Liu Bang, the first emperor of China   military officer and twenty

black dwarfs (as asked for by the merchant, who knew that curiosities of this type were desirable and expensive items in Rome). How reliable any of these accounts are is anyone's guess. Although it does suggest that a few stray traders managed to get as far as China, this does not mean that any official Roman embassy was ever sent.

One curious piece of possible contact relates to a large band of Roman soldiers who were captured after the defeat by the Persians at the Battle of Carrhae in 54 BC. An estimated ten thousand of these Roman prisoners of war may have been deployed as mercenaries on the eastern frontiers of the Persian empire. From there, either by being captured or by escaping, it is possible that some ended up fighting for one of the small warrior states bordering the Han empire. A Chinese history describes how in 36 BC some Han empire soldiers were fighting one of these states and encountered about a hundred men fighting in a 'fish-scale' formation. Anyone who knows anything about Roman fighting techniques will be familiar with what the Romans called the 'Testudo' – the tortoise formation – where a group of soldiers all raised their long shields to form a protective shell over the entire unit. Had this Roman tortoise managed to make it as far as the Chinese borders?

The theory went further. After these 'Romans' had been captured by the Chinese, it was claimed that they were settled in a new village called Liqian, perhaps from 'Legio' for Legion. Scientists actually performed some DNA testing of the village's modern-day inhabitants to see if they had high levels of western genes. The population as a whole showed no difference from the general Chinese population but there were a few individuals who had predominately Caucasian genes. Whether these are the distant descendants of a wandering band of Roman soldiers is another matter. They could easily be the result of a couple of western traders along the silk route marrying local women. Or were they descendants of Alexander's army who still fought in the western manner? To date there has been no other archaeological evidence to support the lost legionaries theory. You would have thought they would have carried some small mementoes with them, or made some Roman-style pots or lamps when they settled down, or perhaps painted pictures of their favourite gladiators to remind themselves of home.

What does comparing Rome and China tell us? They developed separately but they were structurally very similar. Both shifted from city-states with citizen armies to unified empires with professional forces located on the borders. They developed hierarchical bureaucracies to manage their provinces and collect the taxes. The money supply was increased significantly in both by means of the state-controlled minting of coins. They shared an interest in counting how many citizens they had in the form of a census. They collected and codified their laws. Both the Roman and Chinese rich got richer (perhaps they always do). In both societies a uniform elite culture complete with its own literary classics was created. Both justified the very existence of their empires by means of divine support. Both saw a shift away from religious systems based on communal values to ones that emphasised the importance of individual ethical conduct and its role in attaining salvation.

But there were some striking differences. The Roman

empire sprawled around the Mediterranean Sea, whereas the Han empire was based around the river valleys of the Hwang Ho and Yangtse. Trade exerted a far greater influence on Roman life than it did within the context of China's conservative agrarianism. Roman power was fundamentally based on the exercise of military control over a widely diverse group of different ethnicities and cultures, whereas the so-called Warring States which preceded the Han empire shared a common language and culture. Comparing two empires the size of Rome and China is clearly a colossal undertaking. Let's look at some of these areas in more detail in order to show how such comparisons can help us to understand the ancient world.

First, the state. Both Rome and China had originally emerged as powers on the edge of an already well-developed culture. Rome had expanded at a time when Alexander's conquests had created a huge area that was, as already discussed, in some sense Hellenised. Both the Romans and the Han were the rough new kids on the block. Unlike the Han, the Romans were still led by aristocrats. These imperial amateurs had no interest in getting their hands dirty in the messy business of actually managing their conquered territories. Unlike China, then, where the central state became better developed and had a sophisticated bureaucracy, Rome continued to rule in a highly delegated, hands-off way even once its empire had gained great size. In the Roman empire, as we have seen, it was the shock of the third-century crisis which finally forced a renunciation of the reliance on this elite class and the introduction of a more rigorous, centralised state. Even so, Diocletian's enlarged

Roman state employed about thirty thousand civilian officials, less than one quarter of the number in China.

War profoundly affected the ways in which the Roman and Han states developed. Before unification under the Han, China consisted of a group of almost permanently warring states, each roughly equal in power. The level of hostilities is striking. One calculation estimates that there were 256 wars between the major states from 656 to 221 BC. Defeat meant total state annihilation. In order to survive, the individual state had to develop ways in which to extract the maximum possible resources from its people. In other words, it taxed them hard. And with the money it raised it could afford to conscript large numbers of peasants into the army. This whole process required the state to have a sophisticated level of bureaucracy, involving a high level of centralisation, to ensure that the taxes and manpower could be managed. During the early republic, Rome had also developed within a multi-state Italy. But Rome had always been dominant in Latium, the region around Rome itself, and as it expanded in Italy it was able to prevent its enemies from combining to threaten it. It had a wide range of largely loyal allies who it could call upon if required. Only once did Rome face the kind of existential threat that was routine in the Warring States of China. For ten years, the Carthaginian general Hannibal marched his army and elephants all over Italy, inflicting heavy defeats on the Romans, but he lacked the military strength to take Rome itself.

The result was that, before Diocletian's reform of the late empire, Rome was never forced to make changes to its institutional governmental structures in the way the

Chinese states had. This doesn't mean that Rome never faced major military challenges. It did. It was able to confront them, though, in more straightforward ways than with wholesale reform, which was required for state survival in China. First, the Romans found it easy to build various alliances among the many different states they engaged with. In China, by contrast, the number of states was limited; they were relatively closed off from the wider world; and they were locked into a zero-sum game in which roughly equal states fought each other to no effect. Second, the Romans adopted a different strategy with regard to building up its manpower. Rather than extract more men from the same pool of citizens, it expanded its citizen base as it conquered. Citizens could be relied upon to be more loyal and to fight more willingly. There was no need to create a more intensified form of bureaucratic government because it was easier for the Romans simply to expand the system they currently had. For the Chinese, stuck in stalemate, this was never an option.

One view which both Roman and Chinese emperors shared about their respective states was that theirs was the best empire in the world. Obviously both knew that their own was not the only empire in existence, but there seems to have been an underlying assumption that it was only a matter of time before total conquest would be achieved. For the Romans, the empire was 'orbis terrarum', the whole world – an attitude which the pope continues to this day when he gives his blessing 'urbi et orbi': to the City of Rome and to the World. In China, their empire was 'the empire of all people under Heaven'. The Chinese themselves call China the 'Central Kingdom'. It is at the heart of things. This shared sense of overarching superiority was not based solely on a belief in the power of their armed forces. Both Chinese and Romans shared a belief that their civilisation was greater, disparaging those cultures beyond their borders as barbarian. Both built great walls to literally and symbolically keep them out.

Roman society was based on legal distinctions of status. You were either a citizen or a slave, a head of the household or a freedman, a man or woman, all of which meant you had different legal rights. This hierarchical mentality was reflected in the degree to which Romans were at ease with the institution of slavery and enjoyed watching brutal forms of entertainment such as gladiatorial combat.

Contrast this situation with the Han empire. Chinese society was based on the free peasant, and slavery was relatively rare. The bureaucrats that governed and collected taxes were scholar-officials who were expected to be able to compose a poem on the spot. All were in theory legally equal under the emperor. Unlike in Rome, where the lower your status the harsher your punishment, in China punishments for a crime were the same regardless of who carried it out (at least in theory, and they were still very cruel by our standards). Loyalty to the emperor was a central tenet of all society, which had the benefit of weakening the old aristocratic order because loyalties bypassed them and went straight to the top. Again, contrast the situation in Rome, where even the emperor had to struggle with the entrenched vested interests of old senatorial families. Perhaps this was one reason why the Roman emperors needed to organise a state cult around themselves, as they struggled to assert their authority over a society that was less cohesive than China's and more socially stratified. Being thought a god could only help in this endeavour. The Han emperors by contrast were able to keep their involvement with the gods more distant.

The Chinese state was involved in all areas of life. Above all it focused on keeping up the sophisticated system of water control, which supported the complex hydraulic agriculture that meant everyone got fed. Such a large task could only ever be achieved by the state, rather than private enterprise or patronage. Even trade was heavily influenced by state monopolies in goods such as salt and wine. Merchants were therefore often obliged to partner the state in their operations and the state took an active interest in enforcing various quality controls. Trade was not simply a means for the individual to try to get rich. A variety of other means existed to move up the social ladder. The army, trade and the bureaucracy were in theory open to all, although again the degree to which this was true in practice was limited.

Rome was far less centralised. The empire was governed by a local, landowning class. When the Romans conquered a region they usually left the local aristocracy in place – at least those who hadn't resisted them too much. These local bigwigs made sure that the existing system continued to work smoothly and delivered the Romans both taxes and social order. It was this class that provided most of the officers and officials that actually kept the empire running. Over time these locals became Romanised. They dressed like Romans, they built themselves villas and took on Roman names. They did this partly because the Roman lifestyle brought many material benefits for those at the upper end of society. Good food, luxury goods and high culture all became widely accessible to these people. But they also did it to display their loyalty to the Roman regime. What better way to show how loyal you were to the Romans than to live like one?

What is much less clear is whether provincial peasants, labourers and artisans were loyal to the Roman empire. Latin and Greek were the languages of government but were not widely used outside of the urban administrative centres. How much did these ordinary people benefit from being part of the Roman world? They got peace, which was no small thing in this period, and they may have got some increase in prosperity. Many were, however, largely cut off from the luxuries the cities had to offer. Their landowners were often the same families that had overseen them before. For these people, the Roman empire represented just a change in management.

You can get some idea of this difference between Chinese and Roman cultures by looking at their folk heroes. Rome had Aeneas, the hero in Virgil's *Aeneid*, who left the ruins of his native Troy and, after numerous hair-raising escapades, settled in Latium and therefore gave rise to the Roman people. By contrast the folk hero of China, the emperor Yu, began the system of flood control, planted wheat and killed two water dragons. Whereas the individual drive of the aristocrat was regarded as the main force behind Roman civilisation, in China what counted was the state's ability to manage the water supply.

This had far-reaching consequences. Because of the size of the Chinese water-management challenge the state was placed in a position far superior to that of any individual. All people were deeply subservient to the will of the government. Even concepts such as property, which seem core to the western way of doing things, were reduced to relative insignificance in the face of this overwhelming need for state interference in order to make civilised life even possible. Property was regarded as an almost anti-social desire that expressed individual greed at the expense of the collective need of the state. Likewise, when everyone was subordinate to the state then differences in class or status had less meaning. Even the most powerful aristocrat was as nothing compared with the centralised authority of the state. Contrast this with Rome, where the republic was so weak in its last decades that individuals such as Julius Caesar could easily hold it to ransom. One aristocrat could be richer than the entire state. Even such state as did exist was organised along the guiding lines of aristocratic competition. Individual nobles were sent out to lead the legions and govern the conquered provinces. They competed vigorously with each other for these posts and the chance to gain glory. This elite energy was seen as the driving force behind Rome's success and civilisation.

Contrast too the type of emperor who sat at the top of the system. The Roman emperor was first and foremost a military leader. He had control over the legions and used this power to back up his claim to legitimacy. He was the head of the legal system and was expected to spend hours deliberating over the legal cases that came before him.

Thousands of petitions were sent to him by quite ordinary citizens even though there was no practical possibility of the emperor ever having the time to respond to them. One case that succeeded in reaching the emperor Trajan lasted for three days, one of which was taken up by no less than ten hours of counsel speeches. This is an extreme example, perhaps, but indicative of the problem.

The Chinese emperor was a man of peace. He was neither judge nor general but the Son of Heaven, whose Forbidden Palace symbolised the harmony between Heaven and Earth that his reign would maintain. For one thing, there was no civil legal system, only a criminal one. It was also typical that the emperor Yu, who killed two dragons, did so without violence. He simply said: 'The ways of man and nature are ordained by heaven so why should we be alarmed at dragons?' In the face of such effortless superiority the dragons just slunk off and died. It was the scholar gentry of the bureaucracy who got their hands dirty and actually ran things. The Confucian scholar Mencius said that an emperor should govern in the same way that you cook a small fish – very lightly. These were not military men. As one of these scholars said to Genghis Khan, 'You can conquer an empire in the saddle but you cannot rule it from there'. For that you need bureaucrats.

One thing that Roman and Han empires shared was a taste for periodic lavish expenditure, which was paid for by the tribute handed over by their subjects. People paid these taxes partly in money but also in goods from the local area, great quantities of which flowed into the administrative centres, reflecting the very cosmopolitanism of the empire itself. Of course the state had no use for all these goods and therefore traded them in the market for other items, a boost to trade that encouraged the inflow of merchandise from regions well beyond the borders of the empire itself. The Chinese imported fine Roman glass and the Romans loved Chinese silk. The huge array of global goods that could be acquired if you had enough money was astonishing. Only a truly great empire could show off such an exotic range, extracted from such a broad area. This was a characteristic the Chinese recognised in the Roman empire. An account written by a Han official, Gan Ying, states that the Roman empire produces, among many other things: gold, silver, precious jewels, pearls, jade, fighting cocks, rhinoceroses, amber, opaque glass, red cinnabar, multicoloured embroideries, and even asbestos cloth.

The key issue for most people, of course, was that they lacked the money to buy this stuff. It was typical of these great empires that they creamed off a surplus from the countless communities they had conquered and then gave it to a small governing class. This elite, whether scholar bureaucrats, local nobles, imperial households or capital cities, then consumed this surplus in an extravagant and high-profile way. One of the effects of this process was to transform the imperial capital into a colossal city. Rome grew to a million inhabitants in the first century BC, a figure no other European city reached until London after the industrial revolution. A principal reason for Rome's rapid growth was that the government gave out subsidised grain to its citizens, which simply attracted more people. These underemployed citizens were then able to spend more time enjoying the many entertainments laid on by the city. While it is true that Rome was a producer of many goods and services, it is also fair to say that the capital became one huge celebration of the whole imperial project.

Emperors also used the surplus to create great pageantry and pomp surrounding their personages, funding, for example, the palaces on the Palatine Hill in Rome and in Beijing's Forbidden City. The Mausoleum of Augustus looks pretty restrained in comparison with the thousands of terracotta soldiers guarding the tomb of the Qin emperor. In both systems, this lavish expenditure worked in a neatly reinforcing circle by glorifying the emperors while showing how deserving they were in the first place.

Such a system was ripe for further exploitation by the very individuals who benefited from it most. The central governments of both Rome and China relied on the elite's cooperation to raise taxes and they had no option but to turn a blind eye when this slipped into corruption. Wastage and graft were endemic. We may elect to see this not as a moral problem, as suggested by the term corruption, but as a mechanism that greased the wheels of government, allowing things to run smoothly for the greater benefit of all. Whether those poor provincials who were on the receiving end would have agreed is another matter.

The systematic comparative study of these empires is in its infancy. The job is made more challenging by the language difficulties involved and the fact that academics tend to study narrow areas rather than empires as a whole. There are some big questions that these comparisons may shed light on: above all, how the different administrative and political systems that each empire evolved – one centralised and dynastic, the other more federal – affected the future development of East and West. In China, there was a steady imperial cycle, with new dynasties establishing themselves for the long term. In the West, the fall of the Roman empire was followed by much smaller successor states and an absence of central empire. The difference in early state formation may therefore have had a significant impact on the paths that East and West took in the following two millennia. It may even have given rise to the Great Divergence, the huge discrepancy between East and West in economic, political and military power that arose in the eighteenth and nineteenth centuries and is only now beginning to be redressed. Comparing the two imperial systems can help us address such questions. And whatever the answers may be, it is clear that these two empires from the ancient past still exert a heavy influence on the shape of the world we live in today.

6

THROUGH CLASSICAL EYES

The ancient world doesn't always seem that relevant now. In a postmodern digital age, the texts of ancient Greece and Rome can easily look like the relics of a long-lost era, useless in contemporary society. But this is a relatively new phenomenon. For most of the fifteen hundred years since the end of antiquity, reading the classic texts from the ancient world was fundamental to learning. Latin was the language of the Roman Catholic Church, which meant that even after the western Roman empire had disappeared the language retained its position at the heart of Europe's cultural life and the education system. Anyone who was anyone thought and wrote in Latin. Influenced by the ideas and arguments of ancient writers, many came to see the world through classical eyes. It's what you might call seeing things with Rome-coloured vision.

In the eighteenth, nineteenth and even into the early twentieth century, classical works were often thought to be all the literature an educated individual needed to read. The highly literate were so soaked in these texts that the classics permeated every aspect of their lives. When looking for inspiration, authority or explanation it seemed perfectly natural to consult an ancient book. It's hard for us to understand how powerful a cultural force this was. Ask most people today what 'classics' refers to and they will probably say the classics of English literature – Jane Austen, Charles Dickens, and the like. Ask a Renaissance man and you would have revealed your lack of education simply by asking. This wasn't just a matter of snobbery. Many people thought the ancient world represented the pinnacle of human civilisation and artistic achievement. They loved their ancient authors in the same way that Shakespeare is often revered today.

Advances in the sciences meant that the ancient world started to become less practically relevant during the industrial revolution. Before that point, if you had wanted to resolve some pressing problem, whether to do with law, medicine, maths or agriculture, you would have first looked in an ancient book. But then, classics had a resurgence. The Victorian age of imperialism saw ancient authors become directly relevant again. They provided all kinds of useful advice on how to manage conquered lands and lowly subjects. The British government recognised this benefit by increasing its reliance on gentleman imperialists to manage its empire. Between 1892 and 1914, 49 per cent of recruits to the elite Indian Civil Service came from Oxford and 30 per cent from Cambridge. Most of those from Cambridge had degrees in mathematics, and most of those from Oxford had degrees in classics, but all had studied at least Latin. (It is extraordinary now to think that, until 1960, both universities still insisted on all applicants for all subjects having studied Latin.)

The mushrooming of public schools in Britain during the late nineteenth century saw much of the middle class exposed to the benefits of classical education. Classics as a subject was also increasingly available to the working classes, with ordinary schools copying the public schools' emphasis on sport and the learning of Latin and Greek. Developments in printing meant that cheap translations became more widely available through the public library network. Suddenly everyone could access Homer in translation. Ordinary people wanted to share in the learning that had hitherto been largely the preserve of the rich. In this way the respect for ancient literature and the influence of classics began to spread.

The pivotal role that classics has played in education has meant that western writers have habitually turned to classical Greek and Roman sources to help them understand and construct images of the world around them, with the ancient past acting as a prism through which to perceive their contemporary reality. Whether the question concerned how to run an empire, what constituted civilised behaviour, or how to be a good human being, the ancient world has often offered the best source for information. Yet reading is not a passive activity. It involves engaging with and reinterpreting the past in the light of current conditions. Victorian imperialists wanted texts that could be seen as legitimating colonial projects, such as the *Odyssey* in which the heroic Odysseus travelled across the known world and beyond in order to fulfil his destiny. During the expansion of commerce in the Renaissance, by contrast, interpretations of the *Odyssey* had focused on the hero's maritime wanderings. In fact, Odysseus can be seen as exile, hero, adventurer or wanderer – the list is potentially endless. The interpretations of classics have built up over generations, each one reflecting the preoccupations of its own age.

Of course ancient texts do not play the dominant role they once did in western education. Since the end of the Second World War and the end of imperialism studying Latin and Greek has again declined. But even though Classics is no longer a core part of the school syllabus it is still ingrained in our culture. As we shall see, it is hard to escape from the classical influence of the past even if you are trying to say something new. It's easy to end up simply defining yourself in opposition to it.

ISLAM

One of the biggest problems that faced medieval Europe was the arrival of Islam. The Arab invasions swept through the lands of the earlier Roman empire and threatened the very heartlands of Christendom. In order to understand this terrifying new force, men of letters instinctively turned to their classical forefathers. The views of the ancient world helped forge the medieval view of Islam. At first glance it's not obvious how classical texts could do this, given that Muhammad wasn't born until the sixth century AD. The Muslim invasions that swept away what was left of antiquity in the Byzantine empire happened even later. But precedents could in fact be found in classical literature for such a phenomenon.

The appearance of a strange new religion from the Near East was nothing new: Christianity itself had emerged from this route. When the Roman empire had become Christian after Constantine's conversion, the border lands with the Persian world remained a melting pot of all kinds of religious groups. There were heretical Christians who refused to accept the idea of the Trinity and there were others who saw Jesus as having two completely separate natures, one human, the other divine. There were Manichees who saw the world and all its inhabitants as merely the battleground between opposing forces of light and darkness (they liked to eat light-filled vegetables like cucumbers and melons to help keep the darkness at bay). And there were Gnostics, 'knowing ones', whose beliefs were so complex that no one really understands what they meant. So Muhammad was certainly not the first alternative religious leader who had emerged from this part of the world. Nor was he the first monotheist who denied that God had the three aspects of the Trinity. Medieval Christian thinkers simply looked up the appropriate refutations of such heretical beliefs in the great books of the early Church fathers. Islam was then simply slotted into a pre-existing framework for dealing with these heresies.

Another way to interpret Islam was to interpret it as being a new kind of ancient paganism. In medieval art Muslims were often shown worshipping various gods, such as Apollo, Jupiter, Diana or, to emphasise their warlike qualities, Mars. Or they were shown adoring Muhammad as if he were a god. It was all designed to show that Islam, far from being a new religion, was actually a reactionary attempt to go back to primitive pagan times.

A common approach was to emphasise the supposed

promiscuity and loose morals of Islam. Some images showed Muslims praying to the well-endowed ancient god of fertility, Priapus. Other writers alleged that Muhammad was a religious fraud who had only ever sought power in order to have opportunities to satisfy his unnatural lusts. There were lots of attempts to link Muslims with Venus, the god of love. Various myths in the Middle Ages promoted the association of Muhammad with homosexuality, prostitution and adultery. All this sexual innuendo drew on the ancient perception of the East as a place of promiscuity, the idea being that the physical heat of the place must necessarily produce 'hot', lusty human beings.

Of course, none of these claims had any basis in evidence. In reality, these nasty images reflected Christianity's weakness in the face of Muslim military power: slagging off their opponents was a way to vent frustration at being beaten. Muslims didn't read these works, naturally, and were never the intended audience. Such abusive texts were aimed at keeping up morale on the home front, like the songs sung about Hitler's alleged single testicle during the height of the Blitz when Britain was on the ropes. It's a type of humour that reflects underlying nervousness about what might happen, especially when there's a real prospect of defeat, and a way of emphasising the importance of sticking together. Muslim victory, it said, would be terrible for everyone.

The net effect was that the Christian image of the Muslim degenerated into a caricature. Islam became the antithesis of Christian values, and was portrayed as a material religion whose followers were in thrall to power, wealth and sex.

Muslims were thought to be naively credulous in believing such an obvious set of lies as those peddled by Muhammad, himself ridiculed as being an epileptic, demon-possessed fraud. The Quran was dismissed as being repetitive and disorderly, lacking the kind of rational logic supposedly found in the Christian Bible. In the 850s, the Spanish writer Paul Alvarus went so far as to present Muhammad as the precursor of the Antichrist, following on from the Roman emperors Nero and Domitian.

The same kind of out-and-out hostility lay behind the Crusades. The urge to crusade is a difficult phenomenon to understand. Like a stag do in Prague or Amsterdam, it reflected a desire both to travel and to show off how macho you were. However, it also expressed a sincere belief in the importance of continuing the Christian struggle against what was seen as a new form of ancient paganism –the crusaders wanted to smash the pagan idols as their forefathers had done. The Muslims were regarded as a scourge sent by God to force the Christians to recover their ancient fervour, a perspective that reduced Islam to a bit-part player in a narrative in which the Christian God's plan for humanity was fulfilled.

Above all, the Muslims were portrayed as being like ancient barbarians: unsophisticated and savage. Just as the Greeks and the Romans had faced an external threat from what they sometimes characterised as uncivilised groups, it was now claimed that the Christians faced a comparable enemy. In a description of Pope Urban II's original call to Crusade, by the twelfth-century English historian William of Malmesbury, the very idea of Crusade is presented as a battle of the civilisations – except that only the Christians were seen as possessing a civilisation. A key part of this supposed Christian superiority was its classical heritage. Christendom claimed to have inherited all that was best about the ancient world, with a duty to protect and recover it from the barbarian Muslims. It made the Crusades seem a natural part of an historical continuity stretching back to the ancient world.

GIBBON'S TURKS

Clearly, before the eighteenth century, attitudes towards Islam had been predominantly, if not entirely, hostile. Much of this negativity can be ascribed to Christian Europe's need to maintain a healthy distance between itself and its greatest military, religious and cultural threat. The successors to the Arab empire, the Ottoman Turks, had reached as far as Vienna in 1529 and again in 1683. Christendom still seemed to be very much under threat. But as Turkish power waned and that of western European nations rose during the eighteenth century, the need to maintain such a hostile stance decreased. It became possible to consider Islam in a more balanced, less aggressive manner. Edward Gibbon was one of the first historians to do this. Making use of better-quality information he portrayed Islam in a far more favourable light. We tend to think of Gibbon's *History of the Decline and Fall of the Roman Empire*, which was published in six volumes between 1776 and 1789, as focusing on the western part of the Roman empire, which ended in 476 AD. In fact

Gibbon's work also covers the whole period of the eastern Roman empire – the Byzantine world – which ended when Constantinople finally fell in 1453 AD. The colossal arc of his Roman history served as a perfect vehicle for discussing the most important issue which faced Britain in Gibbon's day: how to maintain an empire.

This was a vital matter. The American colonies were in revolt, and by the time of the publication of Gibbon's work they had managed to attain their independence. As a result, what is sometimes called the first British empire had hit a brick wall. If Britain were to regain its imperial momentum, acquire new territories and then manage to hang on to them, it would have to learn from the mistakes of Rome's imperial past.

Morality sat at the heart of Gibbon's view of how this could be achieved. Moral character lay at the core of good government and functioned as a prime mover in the rise and fall of nations. Gibbon's image of decline and fall, therefore, made it clear that the British would have to think about their own morals if they wanted their empire to survive. In Gibbon's view, the period of Rome's decline had seen an increase in luxury and corruption stemming from the immoderate greatness of its empire. This had resulted in a loss of liberty and a move towards absolute monarchy. In Gibbon's time, London itself had developed a fascination with the East and its products on account of the growing trade contacts Britain had established there. Public interest was so high that the Royal Academy of Music appears to have subsidised operas with oriental themes, such as Handel's *Giulio Cesare* (Julius Caesar) and *Serse* (Xerxes), because many of its members had investments in the East India Company, and staging such works acted as a great marketing tool. Gibbon's stark warning was that the flow of wealth and power to Britain from its overseas acquisitions and business interests posed a direct moral threat to the survival and health of the state.

Gibbon loved the ancient world. As a young man he had spent long hours studying the works of Cicero and Tacitus. He saw great benefit in students learning the 'perfect idioms of Rome and Greece'. The ancient world, for Gibbon, was a world of 'light and science', where men 'spoke the sublime language of eloquence and reason'. But Gibbon was far more than just a traditionalist: he wanted to use the classics in order to better understand the modern world. Rather than simply write a chronicle of events, Gibbon used Roman history to get at the root causes of why the world was like it was. Drawing parallels and comparisons with antiquity could generate a better idea of what could happen in the future. For however much Gibbon loved Rome and its civilisation, he realised that the Roman empire could have been derailed far earlier in its history. It was this fragility that was perhaps the main lesson for Gibbon's readers: that the progress that had been attained in the eighteenth century could not be relied upon to continue indefinitely or inevitably. Civilised Europe, under the Romans, had fallen before to the forces of barbarism, and it could not be ruled out that it would fall again. In fact, the fall of so great a civilisation as Rome's served only to emphasise just how possible it was that such a collapse could happen in Europe again.

The battle between civilisation and barbarism is at the

heart of Gibbon's account of the rise of Islam. His barbarians are based on Tacitus's account of the ancient Germans:
they are nomads who lack the civilised arts, laws, property and money. The problem with barbarism in Gibbon's
view was not simply this lack of refined culture. It was that
barbarians are warlike: great warriors who, like the Goths,
could even humble Rome on the battlefield. But while
victory brought great rewards, it in turn led to softness and
a decline in military prowess, leaving the victors themselves
vulnerable to the next barbarian force. Barbarism was, in
this view, nothing but a merry-go-round of violence. It was
this softening of strength, both military and moral, that had
had brought Rome low and Gibbon was keen for Britain to
avoid such a fate.

Gibbon hated religious fanaticism. He saw the great
moral figures of Rome's history as the product of a state that
was unrestrained by the church. Religion, as Gibbon saw it,
could only ever result in sycophancy and servility. People
would be far more willing to accept tyranny and accept
loss of liberty if they were in awe of their religious-political
leaders. Civilisation stood in direct opposition to militant
religion, whether Christian or Muslim. It was religious
fanaticism that had weakened the Roman empire and left
it vulnerable to attack. It was sectarian infighting between
different Christian groups that had so weakened the Byzantine state that it could be swept away by the Arab invasions.
In Gibbon's account, Rome's failings are the mirror image
of Islam's strengths. Islam was a religion that had retained
its purity and was unencumbered by a priestly caste or top-
heavy church institution.

For all Gibbon's attempts to show the British the lessons of Roman history, he deeply distrusted empire. Empire would always tend towards a loss of liberty and a decline in civilised life. This is what made Rome so worthy of Gibbon's admiration: only the Roman empire had managed to balance the demands of law, liberty and empire for so long. Gibbon was greatly reassured that he could also see the Roman political structure reflected in the famously mixed British constitutional settlement, which balanced the needs of the monarch, the aristocracy and the people. The problem with empire was that it ossified society. In Gibbon's view, it took international competition to generate progress, a situation that had been best observed in ancient Greece and republican Rome. By contrast, the power and wealth that came with empire encouraged flattery and sycophancy and so weakened society's constraints on its leaders.

The emperors Diocletian and Constantine had transformed the Roman world into despotism. For Gibbon, the free spirit of Rome was turned into the blind faith of theocracy, and early Christianity was changed from a humble religion of the downtrodden into a hotbed of high politics. But the Crusades themselves represented the ultimate fall of the Roman world into a more general barbarism. The crusaders, who saw their foe as the barbarians, were now characterised by Gibbon as the uncivilised force. His account of the Crusades, which were driven by a savage fanaticism, shows that barbarism had simply become Christianised. Gibbon would have opted for a pre-Christian Roman civilisation every time.

OF FOREIGN WARS

The 1860s building in King Charles Street in London's Whitehall that is home to the British Foreign and Commonwealth Office is a fine example of high imperial art. The anxiety of Gibbon is here replaced by a proud assertion of the morality and permanence of British rule. But is the message of the building as simple as that?

Part of the problem is that we are overly familiar with the classical style. Whether it's the ancient statues in the British Museum, or indeed the building of the museum itself, we are at home with Corinthian columns, pedestals and all the other standard architectural expressions associated with the classical. We think we get it. Indeed it is always tempting to think that we see things in the same way as the ancients did.

The British Foreign and Commonwealth Office

When we look at the Venus de Milo, for example, aren't we looking at the same object (minus her arms that is)? Isn't her essence unchanged and eternal? Well, it's the same piece of marble. This doesn't mean, however, that we understand how it was seen by its ancient viewers – it may, as we have seen, have been painted. If you saw a Latin word printed on the wall of a museum you wouldn't expect to understand it unless you had studied the language. But works of art and buildings are sometimes assumed to be immediately legible, as if our contemporary visual language is the same as that of the ancients. This is optimistic to say the least.

The reality is that classical references have many levels of meaning: what they meant to the ancients; what they meant to those later Britons who incorporated them into their museums and their buildings; and finally, what they mean to us. Understanding a piece of neoclassical architecture means picking apart these different strands.

At first glance, then, the grand and lofty Foreign Office building can seem like just another public building that uses the classical style to establish its authority and importance. Designed by the great architect George Gilbert Scott, it's definitely an impressive building. Scott actually proposed a Gothic design but he was overruled by the then Prime Minister, Lord Palmerston (Scott was able to put his Gothic ideas to use in building the fine hotel at St Pancras station). But why was the government adamant that it wanted a classical building in the 1860s? Firstly, the aim was to proclaim Britain's status within the continent. Britain had, after all, been a part of the Roman empire and to advertise this link was to say loud and clear that Britain was a part of Europe.

More importantly, it was a way of declaring that Britain was the world's leading imperial power, dominant just as the Roman empire had been in its day.

At the time, the complex of buildings was occupied by the Foreign, Colonial, and Home offices, and by the India Office, its separation indicative of just how important a part India played in the British conception of its empire. It was built in the years following the 1857 Indian Mutiny, as the British called the Indian Rebellion, which had come very close to overthrowing British rule in the subcontinent and had resulted in the transference of the burden of administration from the East India Company to the British state. The India Office was built in the same classical manner but was ornamented with sculptures of some of the Indian peoples, including an Afghan, a Gurkha (spelt 'Goorka' on the statue) and a Malay. These were the groups the British saw as having a significant impact on their ability to rule India. The Gurkhas helped control it, the Malays helped run it and the Afghans threatened it. The Colonial Office, which oversaw the administration of other colonies and dominions, had as its centrepiece a giant statue of Britannia dressed as an upper-class Roman woman, surrounded by classical figures stamped with the words 'Knowledge', 'Enlightenment', and 'Power'. Works such as these made a clear statement that the British thought they knew best how to rule India, and indeed the quarter of the globe that it occupied. They exuded an air of permanence, proclaiming that, whatever short-term impact the Mutiny/Rebellion had had, the British were in India to stay. Their rule would be as long-lasting as the marble from which these figures were hewn. Above all they proclaimed 'Power'. Like Rome, Britain's authority could not be challenged by anyone.

But the reality was very different. The events of 1857 had actually shown just how shaky was Britain's hold on the vast Indian territory. It relied on the cooperation of local leaders and minority populations who served in the armed forces, particularly after the Mutiny/Rebellion when recruitment focused on groups such as the Gurkhas and Sikhs, who had remained loyal. The number of ethnic British troops and officers in India was tiny compared with the size of the local population. At the same time Britain was facing increased competition from other European powers on the continent. Germany, in particular, was reunifying. The grand buildings of what is now the Foreign and Commonwealth Office were an attempt to downplay the size of this threat. And as the threats grew bigger so too did the scale of the classically inspired buildings. Lutyens' building in the 1920s of a lavish new imperial capital, New Delhi, with its great domes and endless classical columns is a prime example. It disguised the new reality of Britain's position in the world: that it was threatened by rising powers such as Germany and nationalist feeling within India itself. However much the ancient world was invoked to try to conceal it, these buildings just showed how insecure Britain felt. Whereas Gibbon had used the comparison with Rome to point to dangers that the empire faced, here it was held up as a shield to hide behind.

After the end of Britain's empire, the way in which people perceived classical buildings like the FCO headquarters changed rapidly. I said above how impressive it is, and I genuinely think it is. Yet in the 1960s when many in Britain felt delighted to have shaken off the burden of empire and the endless emphasis on duty, there was a proposal to demolish the entire complex, and indeed most of Whitehall, and start again with a clean slate. The future was bright and the past was just so uncool.

Global leadership had shifted to the US by then. Until the 1960s Washington's buildings had reflected the European taste for neoclassical architecture. The Washington Monument and the Lincoln Memorial both had their roots in the classical past. The Washington Monument, completed in 1888, took 40 years to build and harked back to the use of Egyptian obelisks in the imperial trophies of Roman

architecture. The Lincoln Memorial, built in 1922, had been modelled on the Parthenon. But defeat in Vietnam raised the difficult issue of how the dead of this unpopular war should be memorialised. A small group of veterans set up the Vietnam Veterans Memorial Fund (VVMF), which staged an open and anonymous competition for a design to be built on a site close to the Lincoln and Washington buildings. The VVMF's only stipulation was that the new memorial should be apolitical about the Vietnam War itself.

The Washington Monument

This was in vain. Vietnam had always been too political an issue for the memorial not to become a matter of fierce debate. The competition was won by a twenty-one-year-old Yale undergraduate, Maya Ying Lin. Lin's design caused an uproar. Tom Carhart, a member of VVMF and holder of two purple hearts, denounced it as 'the most insulting and demeaning memorial to our experiences that was possible'. It was, he said, a 'black gash of shame'. Lin was born and raised in America but came to be seen as an Asian outsider. What outraged many critics above all was that the planned memorial substituted what they perceived as a passive Asian aesthetic for the classical codes of heroism of traditional monuments such as the Washington and the Lincoln buildings; a dreadful irony, given that the war had taken place in Indochina.

At first glance it is easy to interpret the memorial as the polar opposite of the classically inspired monuments beside it. Its black stone sinks into the earth, whereas the older monuments' white stone thrusts upwards so as to be seen from a distance. Gone is the heroism of traditional classical monuments. The individuality of the dead soldiers is emphasised by their names being carved at a level that makes them both easily readable and touchable. Its critics saw it as an architectural castration that mirrored the emasculation America had symbolically suffered in losing the war.

Yet the Vietnam memorial still reveals many classical influences. Its central axis points towards both the Washington and Lincoln memorials. Its polished black walls reflect the viewer's own reflection and the Washington

Monument's Egyptian obelisk, both superimposed on the names of the dead. The effect is to link the Vietnam conflict to both the imperial wars and the republican ideals of the past. The image of the foreign obelisk reminds the visitor of the perils of overseas confrontation but Washington also calls to mind the political ideals that can make such adventures so attractive in the first place. The architect deliberately wanted the names of the victims to read like an epic Greek poem, so they are listed not alphabetically but in the chronological order of their deaths. Although at first glance unheroic in form, the memorial does in fact successfully re-establish the heroic individualism of the victims. Like Hector and Achilles, the fallen deserve their place in a chronicle that does not seek to repackage their death in pursuit of a political agenda, but rather lets their part in the narrative speak for itself. Even the black stone reflected some classical motivation. Lin chose it because classical Greek temples were, as we saw earlier, never white but rather highly coloured – that classical architecture had to be white was a later western interpretation. The memorial's black stone was not simply a rejection of traditional notions of the classical but an attempt to understand it more accurately. In questioning the very meaning of the classical the memorial tried to express a far more multicultural image of American identity. It rejected the idea of seeing the world in the black and white terms of moral absolutism. Even the heroes could now be commemorated in black. The racial significance of this hardly needs emphasising when so great a proportion of the dead were black Americans.

We might like to think that the modern world has moved on from the ancient past, that we are free of its influences and prejudices, but we will always be drawn back by the powerful pull of its ideas and the resonance these have had through the centuries. Even if we try to reject the classical world we can end up simply redefining our position in relation to it.

You might think that the ancient world is dead and buried. You might not notice it in your everyday life. But it's still there. If you can't see it it's because you're not looking for it. Once you do you'll realise just how all-pervasive it is. Or at least how widespread is a later reinvention of it. Whether it is the perception of Islam, civilisation or architecture, the way we see can still be affected by the accumulated views and classical interpretations of those who have seen before us. That's where studying the ancient world can help. It lets us see the distortions in our way of seeing. It can help us try to correct them. It might even let us see things clearly for what they are. But what it definitely shows is that we still see, if no longer through classical eyes, then with classically framed vision.

ILLUSTRATIONS

CHAPTER 1: ANOTHER ANCIENT WORLD

Page 3: A painted reconstruction of a statue from the Temple of Aphaea on Aegina. Wikicommons: Glyptothek Munich.

Page 11: The punishment of a slave. A portion of the Big Game Hunt, mosaic in the ambulatory of the Villa del Casale, Piazza Armerina, Sicily, Italy (3–4 CE). Photo: Erich Lessing/Art Resource, NY.

Page 19: A character with the beard and giant erect phallus of Priapus from Pompeii. Museo Archeologico Nazionale (Naples), Italy.

CHAPTER 2: THE ANCIENT WORLD FROM BELOW

Page 22: Market scene. Relief sculpture, Ostia. Museo Ostiense, Ostia Antica, Italy Inv. 134. Photo: Schwanke (neg. 1980.3236). Courtesy of the Deutsches Archäologisches Institut, Rome.

Page 41: Woman in childbirth. Funerary relief from tomb 100, Isola Sacra, Ostia Antica. Photo courtesy of the Deutsches Archäologisches Institut, Rome.

CHAPTER 3: WHAT, WHEN AND WHERE IS THE ANCIENT WORLD?

Page 46: Marble bust of Alexander the Great, said to be from Alexandria, Egypt. Wikicommons: British Museum. Photo © Andrew Dunn 2004.

Page 49: Map of the Hellenistic World at the time of Alexander the Great. Drawn by Martin Lubikowski, ML Design.

Page 57: The Emperor Diocletian. Istanbul Archaeological Museum. Wikicommons: photo by Giovanni dall'Orto.

Page 59: Map of the Roman Empire under Diocletian. Drawn by Martin Lubikowski, ML Design.

CHAPTER 4: HOW DO WE DISCOVER IT?

Page 72: The Barbegal aqueduct. Wikicommons.
Page 78: A mosaic of a skeleton from Pompeii. Museo Archeologico.
Nazionale (Naples), Italy. Photo by Marie-Lan Nguyen.

CHAPTER 5: DID GREECE AND ROME MATTER?

Page 98: Relief of the Persian king Xerxes in the doorway of his palace at
Persepolis. Wikicommons: photo by Jona Lendering.
Page 105: Liu Bang, the first emperor of China. Wikicommons.

CHAPTER 6: THROUGH CLASSICAL EYES

Page 131: The British Foreign and Commonwealth Office in London.
Wikicommons: photo by Lox Pycock.
Page 135: The Washington Monument, Washington DC. Wikicommons:
released by US Navy. Photo by USAF Tech. Sgt. Andy Dunaway.

FURTHER INVESTIGATIONS

CHAPTER 1: ANOTHER ANCIENT WORLD

- On the different experience of the senses in the ancient world, including their use in ancient medicine, see the various articles in Jerry Toner (ed.), *A Cultural History of the Senses in Antiquity* (Bloomsbury, 2014). On colour in particular: Mark Bradley, *Colour and Meaning in Ancient Rome* (Cambridge University Press, 2009).
- The best accounts of what daily life was like in an ancient city are: Mary Beard, *Pompeii: the Life of a Roman Town* (Profile, 2008), Keith Hopkins, *A World Full of Gods* (Weidenfeld & Nicolson, 1999), and Nicholas Horsfall, *The Culture of the Roman Plebs* (Bristol Classical Press, 2003).
- For an analysis of the games in the Roman world: Jerry Toner, *The Day Commodus Killed a Rhino: Understanding the Roman Games* (Johns Hopkins University Press, 2014).
- The best introductions to ancient Greece are: Robin Osborne (ed.), *Classical Greece: 500–323 BC* (Oxford University Press, 2000), and Paul Cartledge (ed.), *The Cambridge Illustrated History of Ancient Greece* (Cambridge University Press, 1998). For Rome, see Peter Garnsey and Richard Saller, *The Roman Empire: Economy, Society and Culture* (University of California Press, 2015), Mary Beard, *SPQR: A History of Ancient Rome* (Profile, 2015), and Greg Woolf, *Rome: An Empire's Story* (Oxford University Press, 2012).
- The Roman nobleman Marcus Sidonius Falx gives an accessible, first-hand introduction to ancient slavery in his manual, *How to Manage Your Slaves* (Profile, 2014).

CHAPTER 2: THE ANCIENT WORLD FROM BELOW

- For the long version of Roman history 'from below': Jerry Toner, *Popular Culture in Ancient Rome* (Polity Press, 2009). For Greece: Sara Forsdyke, *Slaves Tell Tales: And Other Episodes in the Politics of Popular Culture in Ancient Greece* (Princeton University Press, 2012).

- Other works which give more details of various aspects of ordinary life: Claire Holleran, *Shopping in Ancient Rome: the Retail Trade in the Late Republic and the Principate* (Oxford University Press, 2012), Kristina Milnor, *Graffiti and the Literary Landscape in Roman Pompeii* (Oxford University Press, 2014), Michael Peachin (ed.), *The Oxford Handbook of Social Relations in the Roman World* (Oxford University Press, 2011), and Mary Harlow and Ray Laurence (eds), *A Cultural History of Childhood and Family in Antiquity* (Bloomsbury, 2014).

CHAPTER 3: WHAT, WHEN AND WHERE IS THE ANCIENT WORLD?

- For an overview of the Hellenistic age: Michael Scott, *From Democrats to Kings: The Brutal Dawn of a New World from the Downfall of Athens to the Rise of Alexander the Great* (Icon, 2009).
- For the late Roman empire: Peter Garnsey and Caroline Humfress, *The Evolution of the Late Antique World* (Orchard Academic, 2001), and Peter Heather, *The Fall of the Roman Empire* (Macmillan, 2005). Christopher Kelly, *Ruling the Later Roman Empire* (Belknap Press of Harvard University Press, 2004), shows the problems of trying to govern a pre-industrial world in a more intensive way.

CHAPTER 4: HOW DO WE DISCOVER IT?

- On the watermills at Barbegal: for an accessible overview, see Trevor Hodge, 'A Roman Factory', *Scientific American* (November 1990), pp. 58–64. For more detailed discussion: Philippe Leveau, 'The Barbegal water mill in its environment: archaeology and the economic and social history of antiquity', *Journal of Roman Archaeology* 9 (1996), pp. 137–53.
- On the sewers, see the forthcoming work by Erica Rowan and Mark Robinson. On the use of pepper in ancient Rome, see Andrew Wallace-Hadrill's article in Jerry Toner (ed.), *A Cultural History of the Senses in Antiquity* (Bloomsbury, 2014).
- Lead contamination is discussed in Duncan Keenan-Jones, 'Lead Contamination in the Drinking Water of Pompeii', in Eric Poehler, Miko Flohr and Kevin Cole (eds), *Pompeii: Art, Industry and Infrastructure* (Oxbow, 2011), pp. 122–39. See also François Retief and Louise Cilliers, 'Lead poisoning in Ancient Rome', *Acta Theologica: Supplementum 7 (2005)*, pp. 147–63.

- On the analysis of ancient bones: for Pompeii, see Estelle Lazer, *Resurrecting Pompeii* (Routledge, 2009), and on the Herculaneum skeletons, Luciano Fattore, Luca Bondioli, Peter Garnsey, Paola Rossi and Alessandra Sperduti, 'The Human Skeletal Remains from Herculaneum: New Evidence from the Excavation of the *Fornici* 7, 8, 9, 10 and 11', Poster session presented at the 81st Annual Meeting of the American Association of Physical Anthropologists (2012). Gladiator wounds are analysed in Karl Grosschmidt and Fabian Kanz, 'Head Injuries of Roman Gladiators', *Forensic Science International* 160 (2006), pp. 207–16.
- On mental health in the ancient world, see chapter two of Jerry Toner, *Popular Culture in Ancient Rome* (Polity, 2009) and William Harris (ed.), *Mental Disorders in the Classical World* (Brill, 2013).

CHAPTER 5: DID GREECE AND ROME MATTER?

- Stanford University's Ancient Chinese and Mediterranean Empires Comparative History Project (ACME) is the place to go for information and for new publications on the comparative history of Rome and China. See, especially, two books edited by Walter Scheidel: *State Power in Ancient China and Rome* (Oxford University Press, 2015) and *Rome and China: Comparative Perspectives on Ancient World Empires* (Oxford University Press, 2009).
- On the idea of universal empire: Peter Bang and Dariusz Kolodziejczyk (eds), *Universal Empire: A Comparative Approach to Imperial Culture and Representation in Eurasian History* (Cambridge University Press, 2012).
- The cultural contacts between ancient Greece and Persia are explored in Seyed Darbandi and Antigoni Zournatzi (eds), *Ancient Greece and Ancient Iran: Cross-cultural Encounters* (National Hellenic Research Foundation, 2006).

CHAPTER 6: THROUGH CLASSICAL EYES

- For a fuller account of the ways in which Classics influenced later perceptions of Islam and the East: Jerry Toner, *Homer's Turk: How Classics Shaped Ideas of the East* (Harvard University Press, 2013).
- Garth Fowden, *Before and After Muhammad: The First Millennium Refocused* (Princeton University Press, 2014) examines the many continuities that existed between the world of late antiquity and the Islamic world that replaced it.

• On the Vietnam Veterans Memorial, see Marita Sturken, *Tangled Memories: The Vietnam War, the AIDS Epidemic, and the Politics of Remembering* (University of California Press, 1997), and Elizabeth Hess, 'Vietnam: Memorial of Misfortune', in *Unwinding the Vietnam War: From War into Peace*, ed. Reese Williams (Real Comet Press, 1987), pp. 262–80.

INDEX

INDEX